REALIS...
AN...
ITS METHODS

Swami Vivekananda

Advaita Ashrama
(PUBLICATION DEPARTMENT)
5 DEHI ENTALLY ROAD · KOLKATA 700 014

Published by
Swami Bodhasarananda
Adhyaksha, Advaita Ashrama
Mayavati, Champawat, Uttarakhand, Himalayas
from its Publication Department, Kolkata
Email : mail@advaitaashrama.org
Website : www.advaitaashrama.org

Twenty-fourth Reprint, August 2012
1M1C

ISBN 978-81-7505-008-2

Printed in India at
Trio Process
Kolkata 700 014

CONTENTS

CONTENTS

STEPS TO REALISATION

(A class-lecture delivered in America.)

First among the qualifications required of the aspirant for Jnana or wisdom, come Shama and Dama, which may be taken together. They mean the keeping of the organs in their own centres without allowing them to stray out. I shall explain to you first what the word 'organ' means. Here are the eyes; the eyes are not the organs of vision but only the instruments. Unless the organs also are present, I cannot see, even if I have eyes. But, given both the organs and the instruments, unless the mind attaches itself to these two, no vision takes place. So, in each act of perception, three things are necessary — first, the external instruments, then the internal organs, and lastly the mind. If any one of them be absent, then there will be no perception. Thus the mind acts through two agencies — one external and the other internal. When I see things, my mind goes out, becomes externalised; but suppose I close my eyes and begin to think, the mind does not go out, it is internally active. But in either case, there is activity of the organs. When I look at you and speak to you, both the organs and the instruments are active. When I close my eyes and begin to think, the organs are active, but not the instruments. Without the activity of these organs, there will be no thought. You will find that none of you can think without some symbol. In the case of the blind man, he has also to think through some figure. The organs of sight and hearing are generally very active. You must bear in mind that by the word 'organ' is meant the nerve-centre in the brain. The eyes and ears are only the instruments of seeing and hearing, and the organs are inside. If the organs are destroyed by any means, even if the eyes or the ears be there, we shall not see or hear. So in order to control the mind, we must first be able to control these organs. To restrain the mind from wandering outward or inward and keep the organs in their respective centres, is what is meant by the words Shama and Dama. Shama consists in not allowing the mind to externalise, and Dama in checking the external instruments.

Now comes Uparati, which consists in not thinking of things of the senses. Most of our time is spent in thinking about sense-objects, things which we have seen or we have heard, which we shall see or shall hear, things which we have eaten or are eating or shall eat, places where we have lived and so on. We think of them or talk of them most of our time. One who wishes to be a Vedantin must give up this habit.

Then comes the next preparation (it is a hard task to be a philosopher!), Titiksha, the most difficult of all. It is nothing less than the ideal forbearance — 'Resist not evil.' This requires a little explanation. We may not resist an evil, but at the same time we may feel very miserable. A man may say very harsh things to me, and I may not outwardly hate him for it, may not answer him back, and may restrain myself from apparently getting angry, but anger and hatred may be in my mind, and I may feel very badly towards that man. That is not non-resistance; I should be without any feeling of hatred or anger, without any thought of resistance; my mind must then be as calm as if nothing had happened. And only when I have got to that state, have I attained to non-resistance and not before. Forbearance of all misery, without even a thought of resisting or driving it out, without even any painful feeling in the mind or any remorse — this is Titiksha. Suppose I do not resist, and some great evil comes thereby: if I have Titiksha, I should not feel any remorse for not having resisted. When the mind has attained to that state, it has become established in Titiksha. People in India do extraordinary things in order to practise this Titiksha. They bear tremendous heat and cold without caring, they do not even care for snow, because they take no thought for the body; it is left to itself, as if it were a foreign thing.

The next qualification required is Shraddha, faith. One must have tremendous faith in religion and God. Until he has it, he cannot aspire to be a Jnani. A great sage once told me that not one in twenty millions in this world believed in God. I asked him why, and he told me, 'Suppose there is a thief in this room, and he gets to know that there is a mass of gold in the next room, and only a very thin partition between the two rooms; what will be the condition of the thief?' I answered, 'He will not be able to sleep at all; his brain will be actively thinking of some means of getting at the gold, and he will think of nothing else.' Then he replied, 'Do you believe that a man could believe in God and not go mad to get Him? If a man sincerely believes that there is that immense, infinite mine of Bliss, and that It can be reached, would not that man go mad in his struggles to reach It?' Strong faith in God and the consequent eagerness to reach Him constitute Shraddha.

Then comes Samadhana or constant practice to hold the mind in God. Nothing is done in a day. Religion cannot be swallowed in the form of a pill. It requires hard and constant practice. The mind can be conquered only by slow and steady practice.

Next is Mumukshutva, the intense desire to be free. Those of you who have read Edwin Arnold's *Light of Asia*, remember his translation of the first sermon of Buddha, where Buddha says,

Ye suffer from yourselves. None else compels.
None other holds you that ye live and die.
And whirl upon the wheel, and hug and kiss
Its spokes of agony,
Its tire of tears, its nave of nothingness.

All the misery we have is of our own choosing; such is our nature. The old Chinaman, who having been kept in prison for sixty years was released on the coronation of a new emperor, exclaimed, when he came out, that he could not live; he must go back to his horrible dungeon among the rats and mice; he could not bear the light. So he asked them to kill him or send him back to the prison, and he was sent back. Exactly similar is the condition of all men. We run headlong after all sorts of misery, and are unwilling to be freed from them. Every day we run after pleasure and before we reach it, we find it is gone, it has slipped through our fingers. Still we do not cease from our mad pursuit, but on and on we go, blinded fools that we are.

In some oil-mills in India, bullocks are used that go round and round to grind the oil-seed. There is a yoke on the bullock's neck. They have a piece of wood protruding from the yoke, and on that is fastened a wisp of straw. The bullock is blindfolded in such a way that it can only look forward, and so it stretches its neck to get at the straw; and in doing so, it pushes the piece of wood out a little further; and it makes another attempt with the same result and yet another and so on. It never catches the straw, but goes round and round in the hope of getting it, and in so doing, grinds out the oil. In the same way you and I who are born slaves to nature, money and wealth, wives and children, and always chasing a wisp of straw, mere chimeras, and going through an innumerable round of lives without obtaining what we seek. The great dream is love; we are all going to love and be loved, we are all going to be happy and never meet with misery, but the more we go towards happiness, the more it goes away from us. Thus the world is going on, society goes on and we, blinded slaves, have to pay for it without knowing. Study your own lives, and find how little of happiness there is in them, and how little in truth you have gained in the course of the wild-goose-chase of the world.

Do you remember the story of Solon and Croesus? The king said to the great sage that Asia Minor was a very happy place. And the sage asked him, 'Who is the happiest man? I have not seen any one very happy.' 'Nonsense,' said Croesus, 'I am the happiest man in the world.' 'Wait, sir, till the end of your life; don't be in a hurry,' replied the sage and went away. In course of time that king was conquered by the Persians, and they ordered him to be burnt alive. The funeral-pyre was prepared and when poor Croesus saw it, he cried aloud, 'Solon! Solon!' On being asked to whom he referred, he told his story, and the Persian emperor was touched and saved his life.

Such is the life-story of each one of us; such is the tremendous power of nature over us. It repeatedly kicks us away, but still we pursue it with feverish excitement. We are always hoping against hope; this hope, this chimera maddens us; we are always hoping for happiness.

There was a great king in ancient India, who was once asked four questions, of which one was: 'What is the most wonderful thing in the world?' 'Hope,' was the answer. This is the most wonderful thing. Day and night we see people dying around us and yet we think we shall not die; we never think that we shall die or that we shall suffer. Each man thinks that success will be his, hoping against hope, against all odds, against all mathematical reasoning. Nobody is ever really happy here. If a man be wealthy and have plenty to eat, his digestion is out of order, and he cannot eat. If a man's digestion be good, and he has the digestive power of a cormorant, he has nothing to put into his mouth. If he be rich, he has no children. If he be hungry and poor, he has a whole regiment of children, and does not know what to do with them. Why is it so? Because happiness and misery are the obverse and reverse of the same coin; he who takes happiness, must take misery also. We all have this foolish idea that we can have happiness without misery, and it has taken such possession of us that we have no control over the senses.

When I was in Boston, a young man came up to me and gave me a scrap of paper on which he had written a name and address, followed by these words: 'All the wealth and all the happiness of the world are yours, if you only know how to get them. If you come to me, I will teach you how to get them. Charge 5 dollars.' He gave me this and said, 'What do you think of this?' I said, 'Young man, why don't you get the money to print this? You have not even enough money to get this printed!'

He did not understand this. He was infatuated with the idea that he could get immense wealth and happiness without any trouble. There are two extremes into which men are running; one is extreme optimism, when everything is rosy and nice and good; the other, extreme pessimism, when everything seems to be against them. The majority of men have more or less undeveloped brains. One in a million we see with a well-developed brain; the rest either have peculiar idiosyncrasies or are monomaniacs.

Naturally we run into extremes. When we are healthy and young, we think that all the wealth of the world will be ours, and when later we get kicked about by society like footballs and get older, we sit in a corner and croak and throw cold water on the enthusiasm of others. Few men know that with pleasure there is pain, and with pain, pleasure; and as pain is disgusting, so is pleasure, as it is the twin-brother of pain. It is derogatory to the glory of man that he should be going after pain, and equally derogatory, that he should be going after pleasure. Both should be turned aside by men whose reason is balanced. Why will not men seek freedom from being played upon? This moment we are whipped, and when we begin to weep, nature gives us a dollar; again we are whipped, and when we weep, nature gives us a piece of gingerbread, and we begin to laugh again.

The sage wants liberty; he finds that sense-objects are all vain and that there is no end to pleasures and pains. How many rich people in the world want to find fresh pleasures! All pleasures are old and they want new ones. Do you not see how many foolish things they are inventing every day, just to titillate the nerves for a moment, and that done, how there comes a reaction? The majority of people are just like a flock of sheep. If the leading sheep falls into a ditch, all the rest follow and break their necks. In the same way, what one leading member of a society does, all the others do without thinking what they are doing. When a man begins to see the vanity of worldly things, he will feel he ought not to be thus played upon or borne along by nature. That is slavery. If a man has a few kind words said to him, he begins to smile, and when he hears a few harsh words, he begins to weep. He is a slave to a bit of bread, to a breath of air, a slave to dress, to patriotism, to country, to name and fame. He is thus in the midst of slavery and the real man has become buried within through his bondage. What you call man is a slave. When one realises all this slavery, then comes the desire to be free; and intense desire comes. If a piece of burning charcoal be placed on a man's head, see how

he struggles to throw it off. Similar will be the struggles
for freedom of a man who really understands that he is
a slave of nature.

We have now seen what Mumukshutva or the desire
to be free is. The next training is also a very difficult one.
Nityanitya-viveka — discriminating between that which
is true and that which is untrue, between the eternal and
the transitory. God alone is eternal, everything else is
transitory. Everything dies; the angels die, men die,
animals die, earths die, sun, moon and stars — all die;
everything undergoes constant change. The mountains
of today were the oceans of yesterday and will be
oceans tomorrow. Everything is in a state of flux; the
whole universe is a mass of change. But there is One
who never changes, and that is God; and the nearer we
get to Him, the less will be the change for us, the less
will nature be able to work on us; and when we reach
Him, and stand with Him, we shall conquer nature, we
shall be masters of these phenomena of nature, and
they will have no effect on us.

You see, if we really have undergone the above
discipline, we really do not require anything else in this
world. All knowledge is within us. All perfection is
already there in the soul. But this perfection has been
covered up by nature; layer after layer of nature is
covering this purity of the soul. What have we to do?
Really we do not develop our souls at all. What can
develop the perfect? We simply take the veil off; and
the soul manifests itself in its pristine purity, its
natural, innate freedom.

Now begins the inquiry; why is this discipline so

necessary? Because religion is not attained through the ears, nor through the eyes, nor yet through the brain. No scriptures can make us religious. We may study all the books that are in the world, yet we may not understand a word of religion or of God. We may talk all our lives and yet may not be better for it; we may be the most intellectual people the world ever saw, and yet we may not come to God at all. On the other hand, have you not seen what irreligious men have been produced from the most intellectual training? It is one of the evils of your Western civilisation that you are after intellectual education alone, and take no care of the heart. It only makes men ten times more selfish, and that will be your destruction. When there is conflict between the heart and the brain, let the heart be followed, because intellect has only one state — reason, and within that intellect works and cannot get beyond. It is the heart which takes one to the highest plane, which intellect can never reach; it goes beyond intellect and reaches to what is called 'inspiration'. Intellect can never become inspired; only the heart, when it is enlightened, becomes inspired. An intellectual, heartless man never becomes an inspired man. It is always the heart that speaks in the man of love; it discovers a greater instrument than intellect can give you, the instrument of inspiration. Just as the intellect is the instrument of knowledge, so is the heart the instrument of inspiration. In a lower state it is a much weaker instrument than intellect. An ignorant man knows nothing, but he is a little emotional by nature. Compare him with a great professor — what wonderful power the latter possesses! But the professor is bound by his intellect, and he can be a devil and an intellectual man at the same time, but the man of heart can never be a devil; no man with emotion was ever a devil. Properly cultivated, the heart can be changed and will go beyond intellect; it will be changed into inspiration. Man will have to go beyond intellect in the end. The knowledge of man, his powers of perception, of reasoning and intellect and heart, all are busy churning this milk of the world. Out of long churning comes butter, and this butter is God. Men of heart get the 'butter,' and the 'buttermilk' is left for the intellectual.

These are all preparations for the heart, for that love, for that intense sympathy appertaining to the heart. It is not at all necessary to be educated or learned to get to God. A sage once told me, 'To kill others one must be equipped with swords and shields, but to commit suicide a needle is sufficient; so to teach others, much intellect and learning are necessary, but not so for your own self-illumination.' Are you pure? If you are pure, you will reach God. 'Blessed are the pure in heart, for they shall see God.' If you are not pure, and you know all the sciences in the world, that will not help you at all; you may be buried in all the books you read, but that will not be of much use. It is the heart that reaches the goal. Follow the heart. A pure heart sees beyond the intellect; it gets inspired; it knows things that reason can never know, and whenever there is conflict between the pure heart and the intellect, always side with the pure heart, even if you think what your heart is doing is unreasonable. When it is desirous of doing good to others, your brain may tell you that is not politic to do so, but follow your heart, and you will find that you make less mistakes than by following your intellect. The pure heart is the best mirror for the reflection of truth, so all these disciplines are for the purification of the heart. And as soon as it is pure, all truths flash upon it in a minute; all truth in the universe will manifest in your heart if you are sufficiently pure.

The great truths about atoms, and the finer elements, and the fine perception of men, were discovered ages ago by men who never saw a telescope, or a microscope, or a laboratory. How did they know all these things? It was through the heart; they purified the heart. It is open to us to do the same today; it is the culture of the heart really, and not that of the intellect that will lessen the misery of the world.

Intellect has been cultured with the result that hundreds of sciences have been discovered, and their effect has been that the few have made slaves of the many — that is all the good that has been done. Artificial wants have been created, and every poor man, whether he has money or not, desires to have those wants satisfied, and when he cannot, he struggles and dies in the struggle. This is the result. Through the intellect is not the way to solve the problem of misery, but through the heart. If all this vast amount of effort had been spent in making men purer, gentler, more forbearing, this world would have a thousandfold more happiness than it has today. Always cultivate the heart; through the heart the Lord speaks, and through the intellect you yourself speak.

You remember in the Old Testament where Moses was told: 'Take off thy shoes from off thy feet, for the place whereon thou standest is holy ground.' We must always approach the study of religion with that reverent attitude. He who comes with a pure heart and a reverent attitude, his heart will be opened; the doors will open for him and he will see the truth.

If you come with intellect only, you can have a little intellectual gymnastics, intellectual theories, but not truth. Truth has such a face that any one who sees that face becomes convinced. The sun does not require any torch to show it; the sun is self-effulgent. If truth requires evidence, what will evidence that evidence? If something is necessary as witness for truth, where is the witness for that witness? We must approach religion with reverence and with love, and our heart will stand up and say, this is truth and this is untruth.

The field of religion is beyond our senses, beyond even our consciousness. We cannot *sense* God. Nobody has seen God with his eyes or ever will see God in his consciousness. I am not conscious of God, nor you, nor anybody. Where is God? Where is the field of religion? It is beyond the senses, beyond consciousness. Consciousness is only one of the many planes in which we work; you will have to transcend the field of consciousness, to go beyond the senses, approach nearer and nearer to your own centre, and as you do that, you will approach nearer and nearer to God. What is the proof of God? Direct perception, Pratyaksha. The proof of this wall is that I perceive it. God has been perceived that way by thousands before and will be perceived by all who want to perceive Him. But this perception is no sense-perception at all; it is super-sensuous, superconscious, and all this training is needed to take us beyond the senses. By means of all sorts of past work and bondages we are being dragged down-ward; these preparations will make us pure and light. Bondages will fall off by themselves, and we shall be buoyed up beyond this plane of sense-perception to which we are tied down, and then we shall see, and hear, and feel things which men in the three ordinary states (viz waking, dream and sleep) neither feel, nor see, nor hear. Then we shall speak a strange language, as it were, and the world will not understand us, because it does not know anything but the senses. True religion is entirely transcendental. Every being that is in the universe has the potentiality of transcending the senses; even the little worm will one day transcend the senses and reach God. No life will be a failure; there is no such thing as failure in the universe. A hundred times man will hurt himself, a thousand times he will tumble, but in the end he will realise that he is God. We know there is no progress in a straight line. Every soul moves, as it were, in a circle, and will have to complete it, and no soul can go so low but there will come a time when it will have to go upwards. No one will be lost. We are all projected from one common centre, which is God. The highest as well as the lowest life God ever projected, will come back to the Father of all lives, 'From whom all beings are projected, in whom all live, and unto whom they all return; this is God.'

HINTS ON PRACTICAL SPIRITUALITY

(Delivered at the Home of Truth, Los Angeles, California.)

This morning I shall try to present to you some ideas about breathing and other exercises. We have been discussing theories so long, now it will be well to have a little of the practical. A great many books have been written in India upon this subject. Just as your people are practical in many things, so it seems our people are practical in this line. Five persons in this country will join their heads together and say, 'We will have a joint-stock company,' and in five hours it is done; in India they could not do it in fifty years; they are so unpractical in matters like this. But, mark you, if a man starts a system of philosophy, however wild its theory may be, it will have followers. For instance, a sect is started to teach that if a man stands on one leg for twelve years, day and night, he will get salvation — there will be hundreds ready to stand on one leg. All the suffering will be quietly borne. There are people who keep their arms upraised for years to gain religious merit. I have seen hundreds of them. And, mind you, they are not always ignorant fools, but are men who will astonish you with the depth and breadth of their intellect. So, you see, the word 'practical' is also relative.

We are always making this mistake in judging others; we are always inclined to think that our little mental universe is all that is; our ethics, our morality, our sense of duty, our sense of utility, are the only things that are worth having. The other day when I was going to Europe, I was passing through Marseilles, where a bull-fight was being held. All the Englishmen in the steamer were mad with excitement, abusing and criticising the whole thing as cruel. When I reached England, I heard of a party of prize-fighters who had been to Paris, and were kicked out unceremoniously by the French, who thought prize-fighting very brutal. When I hear these things in various countries, I begin to understand the marvellous saying of Christ: 'Judge not that ye be not judged.' The more we learn, the more we find out how ignorant we are, how multiform and multisided is this mind of man. When I was a boy, I used to criticise the ascetic practices of my countrymen; great preachers in our own land have criticised them; the greatest man that was ever born, Buddha himself criticised them. But all the same, as I am growing older, I feel that I have no right to judge. Sometimes I wish that, in spite of all their incongruities, I had one fragment of their power to do and suffer. Often I think that my judgment and my criticism do not proceed from any dislike of torture, but from sheer cowardice, because I cannot do it, I dare not do it.

Then you see that strength, power and courage are things which are very peculiar. We generally say, 'A courageous man, a brave man, a daring man'; but we must bear in mind that that courage or bravery or any other trait does not always characterise the man. The same man who would rush to the mouth of a cannon shrinks from the knife of the surgeon; and another man who never dares to face a gun, will calmly bear a severe surgical operation, if need be. Now, in judging others you must always define your terms of courage or greatness. The man whom I am criticising as not good, may be wonderfully so in some points in which I am not.

Take another example. You often note, when people are discussing as to what man and woman can do, always the same mistake is made. They think, they show man at his best because he can fight, for instance, and undergo tremendous physical exertion; and this is pitted against the physical weakness and the non-combating quality of woman. This is unjust. Woman is as courageous as man. Each is equally good in his or her way. What man can bring up a child with such patience, endurance, and love as the woman can? The one has developed the power of doing; the other the power of suffering. If woman cannot act, neither can man suffer. The whole universe is one of perfect balance. I do not know, but some day we may wake up and find that the mere worm has something which balances our manhood. The most wicked person may have some good qualities that I entirely lack. I see that every day of my life. Look at the savage! I wish I had such a splendid physique. He eats, he drinks, to his heart's content, without knowing perhaps what sickness is, while I am suffering every minute. How many times would I have been glad to have changed my brain for his body! The whole universe is only a wave and a hollow; there can be no wave without a hollow. Balance everywhere. You have one thing great, your neighbour has another thing great. When you are judging man and woman, judge them by the standard of their respective greatness. One cannot be in the other's shoes. The one has no right to say that the other is wicked. It is the same old superstition that says, 'If this is done, the world will go to ruin.' But in spite of this the world has not yet come to ruin. It was said in this country that if the Negroes were freed, the country would go to ruin — but did it? It was also said that if the masses were educated, the world would come to ruin — but it was only made better. Several years ago a book came out depicting the worst thing that could happen to England. The writer showed that as workmen's wages were rising, English commerce was declining. A cry was raised that the workmen in England were exorbitant in their demands, and that the Germans worked for less wages. A commission was sent over to Germany to investigate this and it reported that the German labourers received higher wages. Why was it so? Because of the education of the masses. Then how about the world going to ruin if the masses are educated? In India, especially, we meet with old fogies all over the land. They want to keep everything secret from the masses. These people come to the very satisfying conclusion that they are the *creme de la creme* of this universe. They believe they cannot be hurt by these dangerous experiments. It is only the masses that can be hurt by them!

Now, coming back to the practical. The subject of the practical application of psychology has been taken up in India from very early times. About 1400 years before Christ, there flourished in India a great philosopher, Patanjali by name. He collected all the facts, evidences, and researches in psychology and took advantage of all the experiences accumulated in the past. Remember, this world is very old; it was not created only two or three thousand years ago. It is taught here in the West that society began 1800 years ago, with the New Testament. Before that there was no society. That may be true with regard to the West, but it is not true as regards the whole world. Often, while I was lecturing in London, a very intellectual and intelligent friend of mine would argue with me, and one day after using all his weapons against me, he suddenly exclaimed, 'But why did not your Rishis come to England to teach us?' I replied, 'Because there was no England to come to. Would they preach to the forests?'

'Fifty years ago,' said Ingersol to me, 'you would have been hanged in this country if you had come to preach. You would have been burned alive or you would have been stoned out of the villages.'

So there is nothing unreasonable in the supposition that civilisation existed 1400 years before Christ. It is not yet settled whether civilisation has always come from the lower to the higher. The same arguments and proofs that have been brought forward to prove this proposition can also be used to demonstrate that the savage is only a degraded civilised man. The people of China, for instance, can never believe that civilisation sprang from a savage state, because the contrary is within their experience. But when you talk of the civilisation of America, what you mean is the perpetuity and the growth of your own race.

It is very easy to believe that the Hindus, who have been declining for 700 years, were highly civilised in the past. We cannot prove that it is not so.

There is not one single instance of any civilisation being spontaneous. There was not a race in the world which became civilised unless another civilised race came and mingled with that race. The origin of civilisation must have belonged, so to say, to one or two races who went abroad, spread their ideas, and intermingled with other races, and thus civilisation spread.

For practical purposes, let us talk in the language of modern science. But I must ask you to bear in mind that, as there is religious superstition, so also there is a superstition in the matter of science. There are priests who take up religious work as their speciality; so also there are priests of physical law, scientists. As soon as a great scientific name, like Darwin or Huxley, is cited, we follow blindly. It is the fashion of the day. Ninety-nine per cent of what we call scientific knowledge are mere theories. And many of them are no better than the old superstitions of ghosts with many heads and hands; but with this difference that the latter differentiated man a little from stocks and stones. True science asks us to be cautious. Just as we should be careful with the priests, so we should be with the scientists. Begin with disbelief. Analyse, test, prove everything, and then take it. Some of the most current beliefs of modern science have not been proved. Even in such a science as mathematics, the vast majority of its theories are only working hypotheses. With the advent of greater knowledge they will be thrown away.

In 1400 B.C. a great sage made an attempt to arrange, analyse and generalise upon certain psychological facts. He was followed by many others who took up parts of what he had discovered and made a special study of them. The Hindus alone of all ancient races took up the study of this branch of knowledge in right earnest. I am teaching you now about it, but how many of you will practise it? How many days, how many months will it be before you give it up? You are impractical on this subject. In India, they will persevere for ages and ages. You will be astonished to hear that they have no churches, no common prayers, or anything of the kind; but they, every day, still practise the breathings and try to concentrate the mind; and that is the chief part of their devotion. These are the main points. Every Hindu must do these. It is the religion of the country. Only, each one may have a special method — a special form of breathing, a special form of concentration, and what is one's special method, even one's wife need not know; the father need not know the son's. But they all have to do these. And there is nothing occult about these things. The word 'occult' has no bearing on them. Near the Ganges thousands and thousands of people may be seen daily sitting on its banks breathing and concentrating with closed eyes. There may be two reasons that make certain practices impracticable for the generality of mankind. One is, the teachers hold that the ordinary people are not fit for them. There may be some truth in this, but it is due more to pride. The second is the fear of persecution. A man, for instance, would not like to practise breathing publicly in this country, because he would be thought so queer; it is not the fashion here. On the other hand, in India, if a man prayed, 'Give us this day our daily bread,' people would laugh at him. Nothing could be more foolish to the Hindu mind than to say, 'Our Father which art in Heaven.' The Hindu, when he worships, thinks that God is within himself.

According to the Yogis there are three principal nerve-currents: one they call the Ida, the other the Pingala, and the middle one the Sushumna, and all these are inside the spinal column. The Ida and the Pingala, the left and the right, are clusters of nerves, while the middle one, the Sushumna, is hollow and is not a cluster of nerves. This Sushumna is closed, and for the ordinary man is of no use, for he works through the Ida and the Pingala only. Currents are continually going down and coming up through these nerves, carrying orders all over the body through other nerves running to the different organs of the body.

It is the regulation and the bringing into rhythm of the Ida and Pingala that is the greater object of breathing. But that itself is nothing—it is only so much air taken into the lungs; except for purifying the blood, it is of no more use. There is nothing occult in the air that we take in with our breath and assimilate to purify the blood; the action is merely a motion. This motion can be reduced to the unit movement we call 'Prana';

and everywhere, all movements are the various manifestations of this Prana. This Prana is electricity, it is magnetism, it is thrown out by the brain as thought. Everything is Prana; it is moving the sun, the moon and the stars.

We say, whatever is in this universe has been projected by the vibration of the Prana. The highest result of vibration is thought. If there be any higher, we cannot conceive of it. The nerves, Ida and Pingala, work through the Prana. It is the Prana that is moving every part of the body, becoming the different forces. Give up that old idea that God is something that produces the effect and sits on a throne dispensing justice. In working we become exhausted because we use up so much Prana.

The breathing exercises, called Pranayama, bring about regulation of the breathing, rhythmic action of the Prana. When the Prana is working rhythmically, everything works properly. When the Yogis get control over their own bodies, if there is any disease in any part, they know that the Prana is not rhythmic there and they direct the Prana to the affected part until the rhythm is re-established.

Just as you can control the Prana in your own body, so, if you are powerful enough, you can control, even from here, another man's Prana in India. It is all one. There is no break; unity is the law. Physically, psychically, mentally, morally, metaphysically, it is all one. Life is only a vibration. That which vibrates this ocean of ether, vibrates you. Just as in a lake, various strata of ice of various degrees of solidity are formed, or as in an ocean of vapour there are various degrees of density, so is this universe an ocean of matter. This is an ocean of ether, in which we find the sun, moon, stars, and ourselves — in different states of solidity; but the continuity is not broken; it is the same throughout.

Now, when we study metaphysics, we come to know the world is one, not that the spiritual, the material, the mental, and the world of energies are separate. It is all one, but seen from different planes of vision. When you think of yourself as a body, you forget that you are a mind; and when you think of yourself as a mind, you will forget the body. There is only one thing, that you are; you can see it either as matter or body, or you can see it as mind or spirit. Birth, life and death are but old superstitions. None was ever born, none will ever die; one changes one's position — that is all. I am sorry to see in the West how much they make of death; always trying to catch a little life. 'Give us life after death! Give us life!' They are so happy if anybody tells them that they are going to live afterwards! How can I ever doubt such a thing? How can I imagine that I am dead? Try to think of yourself as dead and you will see that you are present to see your own dead body. Life is such a wonderful reality that you cannot for a moment forget it. You may as well doubt that you exist. This is the first fact of consciousness — I am. Who can imagine a state of things which never existed? It is the most self-evident of all truths. So, the idea of immortality is inherent in man. How can one discuss a subject that is unimaginable? Why should we want to discuss the *pros* and *cons* of a subject that is self-evident?

The whole universe, therefore, is a unit, from whatever standpoint you view it. Just now, to us, this universe is a unit of Prana and Akasa, force and matter. And mind you, like all other basic principles, this is also self-contradictory. For what is force? — that which moves matter. And what is matter? — that which is moved by force. It is a seesaw! Some of the fundamentals of our reasoning are most curious, in spite of our boast of science and knowledge. 'It is a headache without a head,' as the Sanskrit proverb says. This state of things has been called Maya. It has neither existence nor non-existence. You cannot call it existence, because that only exists which is beyond time and space, which is self-existent. Yet this world satisfies to a certain degree our idea of existence. Therefore it has an apparent existence.

But there is the real existence in and through everything; and that reality, as it were, is caught in the meshes of time, space and causation. There is the real man, the infinite, the beginningless, the endless, the ever blessed, the ever free. He has been caught in the meshes of time, space and causation. So has everything in this world. The reality of everything is the same Infinite. This is not idealism; it is not that the world does not exist. It has a relative existence, and fulfils all its requirements. But it has no independent existence. It exists because of the Absolute Reality beyond time, space and causation.

I have made long digressions. Now, let us return to our main subject.

All the automatic movements and all the conscious

movements are the working of Prana through the nerves. Now, you see, it will be a very good thing to have control over the unconscious actions.

On some other occasion I told you the definition of God and man. Man is an infinite circle, whose circumference is nowhere, but the centre is located on one spot, and God is an infinite circle, whose circumference is nowhere but whose centre is everywhere. He works through all hands, sees through all eyes, walks on all feet, breathes through all bodies, lives in all life, speaks through every mouth, and thinks through every brain. Man can become like God and acquire control over the whole universe, if he multiplies infinitely his centre of self-consciousness. Consciousness, therefore, is the chief thing to understand. Let us say that here is an infinite line amid darkness. We do not see the line, but on it there is one luminous point which moves on. As it moves along the line, it lights up its different parts in succession, and all that is left behind becomes dark again. Our consciousness may well be likened to this luminous point. Its past experiences have been replaced by the present or have become subconscious. We are not aware of their presence in us; but there they are, unconsciously influencing our body and mind. Every movement that is now being made without the help of consciousness was previously conscious. Sufficient impetus has been given to it to work of itself.

The great error in all ethical systems, without exception, has been the failure of teaching the means by which man could refrain from doing evil. All the systems of ethics teach, 'Do not steal!' Very good; but why does a man steal? Because all stealing, robbing and other evil actions, as a rule, have become automatic. The systematic robber, thief, liar, unjust man and woman, are all these in spite of themselves! It is really a tremendous psychological problem. We should look upon man in the most charitable light. It is not so easy to be good. What are you but mere machines until you are free? Should you be proud because you are good? Certainly not. You are good because you cannot help it. Another is bad, because he cannot help it. If you were in his position, who knows what you would have been? The woman in the street, or the thief in the jail, is the Christ that is being sacrificed that you may be a good man. Such is the law of balance. All the thieves and the murderers, all the unjust, the weakest, the wickedest, the devils, they all are my Christ! I owe a worship to the God-Christ and to the demon-Christ! That is my doctrine, I cannot help it. My salutation goes to the feet of the good, the saintly, and to the feet of the wicked and the devilish! They are all my teachers, all are my spiritual fathers, all are my Saviours. I may curse one and yet benefit by his failings; I may bless another and benefit by his good deeds. This is as true as that I stand here. I have to sneer at the woman walking in the street, because society wants it! She, my Saviour, she, whose street-walking is the cause of the chastity of other women! Think of that. Think, men and women, of this question in your mind. It is a truth — a bare bold truth! As I see more of the world, see more of men and women, this conviction grows stronger. Whom shall I blame?

Whom shall I praise? Both sides of the shield must be seen.

The task before us is vast; and first and foremost, we must seek to control the vast mass of sunken thoughts which have become automatic with us.

The evil deed is, no doubt, on the conscious plane, but the cause which produced the evil deed was far beyond in the realms of the unconscious, unseen and therefore more potent.

Practical psychology directs first of all its energies in controlling the unconscious, and we know that we can do it. Why? Because we know the cause of the unconscious is the conscious; the unconscious thoughts are the submerged millions of our old conscious thoughts. Old conscious actions become petrified — we do not look at them, do not know them, have forgotten them. But mind you, if the power of evils is in the unconscious, so also is the power of good. We have many things stored in us as in a pocket. We have forgotten them, do not even think of them, and there are many of them, rotting, becoming positively dangerous; they come forth, the unconscious causes which kill humanity. True psychology would, therefore, try to bring them under the control of the conscious. The great task is to revive the whole man, as it were, in order to make him the complete master of himself. Even what we call the automatic action of the organs within our bodies, such as the liver etc., can be made to obey our commands.

This is the first part of the study, the control of the unconscious. The next is to go beyond the conscious.

Just as unconscious work is beneath consciousness, so there is another work which is above consciousness. When this superconscious state is reached, man becomes free and divine; death becomes immortality, weakness becomes infinite power, and iron bondage becomes liberty. That is the goal, the infinite realm of the superconscious.

So, therefore, we see now that there must be a twofold work. First, by the proper working of the Ida and the Pingala, which are the two existing ordinary currents, to control the subconscious action; and secondly, to go beyond even consciousness.

The books say that he alone is the Yogi who, after long practice in self-concentration, has attained to this truth. The Sushumna now opens and a current which never before entered into this new passage will find its way into it and gradually ascend to (what we call in figurative language) the different lotus-centres, till at last it reaches the brain. Then the Yogi becomes conscious of what he really is, God Himself.

Every one without exception, every one of us, can attain to this culmination of Yoga. But it is a terrible task. If a person wants to attain to this truth, he will have to do something more than listen to lectures and take a few breathing exercises. Everything lies in the preparation. How long does it take to strike a light? Only a second; but how long it takes to make the candle! How long does it take to eat a dinner? Perhaps half an hour. But hours to prepare the food! We want to strike the light in a second, but we forget that the making of the candle is the chief thing.

But though it is so hard to reach the goal, yet even our smallest attempts are not in vain. We know that nothing is lost. In the Gita Arjuna asks Krishna, 'Those who fail in attaining perfection in Yoga in this life, are they destroyed like the clouds of summer?' Krishna replies, 'Nothing, my friend, is lost in this world. Whatever one does, that remains as one's own, and if the fruition of Yoga does not come in this life, one takes it up again in the next birth.' Otherwise, how do you explain the marvellous childhood of Jesus, Buddha, Sankara?

Breathing, posturing, etc. are, no doubt, helps in Yoga; but they are merely physical. The great preparations are mental. The first thing necessary is a quiet and peaceable life.

If you want to be a Yogi, you must be free, and place yourself in circumstances where you are alone and free from all anxiety. He who desires a comfortable and nice life and at the same time wants to realise the Self, is like the fool who wanting to cross the river, caught hold of a crocodile, mistaking it for a log of wood. 'Seek ye first the kingdom of God, and everything shall be added unto you!' This is the one great duty, this is renunciation. Live for an ideal, and leave no place in the mind for anything else. Let us put forth all our energies to acquire that which never fails — our spiritual perfection. If we have true yearning for realisation, we must struggle, and through struggle growth will come. We shall make mistakes, but they may be angels unawares.

The greatest help to spiritual life is meditation

(Dhyana). In meditation we divest ourselves of all material conditions and feel our divine nature. We do not depend upon any external help in meditation. The touch of the soul can paint the brightest colour even in the dingiest places; it can cast a fragrance over the vilest thing; it can make the wicked divine — and all enmity, all selfishness is effaced. The less the thought of the body, the better. For it is the body that drags us down. It is attachment, identification, which makes us miserable. That is the secret. To think that I am the spirit and not the body, and that the whole of this universe with all its relations, with all its good and all its evil, is but as a series of paintings — scenes on a canvas — of which I am the witness.

THE WAY TO BLESSEDNESS

I shall tell you a story from the Vedas tonight. The Vedas are the sacred scriptures of the Hindus and are a vast collection of literature, of which the last part is called the Vedanta, meaning the end of the Vedas. It deals with the theories contained in them, and more especially the philosophy with which we are concerned. It is written in archaic Sanskrit, and you must remember it was written thousands of years ago. There was a certain man who wanted to make a big sacrifice. In the religion of the Hindus, sacrifice plays a great part. There are various sorts of sacrifices. They make altars and pour oblations into the fire, and repeat various hymns and so forth; and at the end of the sacrifice they make a gift to the Brahmins and the poor. Each sacrifice has its peculiar gift. There was one sacrifice, where everything a man possessed had to be given up. Now this man, though rich, was miserly, and at the same time wanted to get a great name for having made this most difficult sacrifice. And when he made this sacrifice, instead of giving up everything he had, he gave away only his blind, lame and old cows that would never more give milk. But he had a son called Nachiketa, a bright young boy, who observing the poor gifts made by his father and pondering on the demerit that was sure to accrue to him thereby, resolved to make amends for them by making a gift of himself. So he went to his father and said, 'And to whom will you give me?' The father did not answer the boy, and the boy asked a second and a third time, when the father got vexed and said, 'Thee I give unto Yama, thee I give unto Death.' And the boy went straight to the kingdom of Yama. Yama was not at home, so he waited there. After three days Yama came and said to him, 'O Brahmana, thou art my guest, and thou hast been here for three days without any food. I salute thee, and in order to repay thee for this trouble, I will grant thee three booms.' Then the boy asked the first boon, 'May my •father's anger against me get calmed down' and the second boon was that he wanted to know about a certain sacrifice. And then came the third boon. 'When a man dies, the question is: what becomes of him? Some people say he ceases to exist. Others say that he exists. This is the third boon that I want. Please tell me what the answer is.' Then Death answered, 'The gods in ancient times tried to unravel the mystery; this mystery is so fine that it is hard to know. Ask for some other boon: do not ask this one. Ask for a long life of a hundred years. Ask for cattle and horses, ask for great kingdom. Do not press me to answer this. Whatever man desires for his enjoyment, ask all that and I will fulfil it, but do not want to know this secret.' 'No sir,' said the boy, 'man is not to be satisfied with wealth; if wealth were wanted we should get it, if we have only seen you. We shall also live so long as you rule. What decaying mortal, living in the world below and possessed of knowledge, having gained the company of the undecaying and the immortal, will delight in long life, knowing the nature of the pleasure produced by song and sport? Therefore, tell me this secret about the great hereafter, I do not want anything else; that is what Nachiketa wants, the mystery of death.' Then the God of Death was pleased.

We have been saying in the last two or three lectures that this Jnana prepares the mind. So you see here that the first preparation is that a man must desire nothing else but the truth, and truth for truth's sake. See how this boy rejected all these gifts which Death offered him — possessions, property, wealth, long life — and everything he was ready to sacrifice for this one idea, knowledge only, the truth. Thus alone can truth come. The God of Death became pleased. 'Here are two ways,' he said, 'one of enjoyment, the other of blessedness. These two in various ways draw mankind. He is the sage who, of these two, takes up that which leads to blessedness, and he degenerates who takes up the road to enjoyment. I praise you, Nachiketa, you have not asked for desires. In various ways I tempted you towards the path of enjoyment; you resisted them all, you have known that knowledge is much higher than a life of enjoyment.

'You have understood that the man, who lives in ignorance and enjoys, is not different from the brute, beast. Yet there are many who, though steeped in ignorance, in the pride of their hearts, think that they are great sages and go round and round in many crooked ways, like the blind led by the blind. This truth, Nachiketa, never shines in the heart of those who are like ignorant children, deluded by a few lumps

of earth. They do not understand this world, nor the
other world. They deny this and the other one, and thus
again and again come under my control. Many have
not even the opportunity to hear about it; and many,
though hearing, cannot know it, because the teacher
must be wonderful; so must he be wonderful too unto
whom the knowledge is carried. If the speaker is a man
who is not highly advanced, then even a hundred times
heard, and a hundred times thought, the truth never
illumines the soul. Do not disturb your mind by vain
arguments, Nachiketa; this truth only becomes
effulgent in the heart which has been made pure. He
who cannot be seen without the greatest difficulty, He
who is hidden, He who has entered the cave of the
heart of hearts, the Ancient One, cannot be seen with
the external eyes, seeing Whom with the eyes of the
soul, one gives up both pleasure and pain. He who
knows this secret gives up all his vain desires, and
attains the superfine perception, and thus becomes
ever-blessed. Nachiketa, that is the way to blessedness.
He is beyond all virtue, beyond all vice, beyond all
duties, beyond all non-duties, beyond all existence,
beyond all that is to be; he who knows this, alone
knows. He Whom all the Vedas seek, to see Whom
men undergo all sorts of asceticism, I will tell you His
name: it is Om. This eternal Om is the Brahman, this
is the immortal One; he who knows the secret of this,
whatever he desires, is his. This Self of man, Nachiketa,
about which you seek to know, is never born, and never
dies. Without beginning, ever existing, this Ancient
One is not destroyed when the body is destroyed. If

the slayer thinks that he can slay, and if the slain man thinks he is slain, both are mistaken, for neither can the Self kill, nor can It be killed. Infinitely smaller than the smallest particle, infinitely greater than the greatest existence, the Lord of all lives in the cave of the heart of every being. He who has become sinless sees Him in all His glory, through the mercy of the same Lord. (We find that the mercy of God is one of the causes of God-realisation). Sitting He goes far, lying He goes everywhere; who else but men of purified and subtle understanding are qualified to know the God in whom all conflicting attributes meet? Without body, yet living in the body, untouched, yet seemingly in contact, omnipresent — knowing the Atman to be such, the sage gives up all misery. This Atman is not to be attained by the study of the Vedas, nor by the highest intellect, nor by much learning. Whom the Atman seeks, he gets the Atman; unto him He discloses His glory. He who is continuously doing evil deeds, he whose mind is not calm, he who cannot meditate, he who is always disturbed and fickle — he cannot understand and realise this Atman who has entered the cave of the heart. This body, O Nachiketa, is the chariot, the organs of the senses are the horses, the mind is the reins, the intellect is the charioteer, and the soul is the rider in the chariot. When the soul joins himself with the charioteer, Buddhi or intellect, and then through it with the mind, the reins, and through it again with the organs, the horses, he is said to be the enjoyer; he perceives, he works, he acts. He whose mind is not under control and who has no discrimination, his senses

are not controllable, like vicious horses in the hands of
a driver. But he, who has discrimination, whose mind
is controlled, his organs are always controllable like
good horses in the hands of a driver. He who has
discrimination, whose mind is always in the way to
understand truth, who is always pure — he receives that
truth, attaining which there is no rebirth. This, O
Nachiketa, is very difficult; the way is long, and it is hard
to attain. It is only those who have attained the finest
perception that can see it, that can understand it. Yet
do not be frightened. Awake, be up and doing. Do not
stop till you have reached the goal. For the sages say
that the task is very difficult, like walking on the edge
of a razor. He who is beyond the senses, beyond all
touch, beyond all form, beyond all taste, the
Unchangeable, the Infinite, beyond even intelligence,
the Indestructible — knowing Him alone we are safe
from the jaws of death.'

So far, we see that Yama describes the goal that is
to be attained. The first idea that we get is that birth,
death, misery and the various tossings about to which
we are subject to in the world can only be overcome by
knowing that which is real. What is real? That which
never changes, the Self of man, the Self behind the
universe. Then, again, it is said that it is very difficult
to know Him. Knowing does not mean simply
intellectual assent, it means realisation. Again and
again we have read that this salvation is to be seen, to
be perceived. We cannot see it with the eyes; the
perception for it has to become superfine. It is gross
perception by which the walls and books are perceived,

but the perception to discern the truth has to be made very fine, and that is the whole secret of this knowledge. Then Yama says that one must be very pure. That is the way to making the perception superfine; and then he goes on to tell us other ways. That self-existent One is far removed from the organs. The organs or instruments see outwards, but the self-existing One, the Self, is seen inwards. You must remember the qualification that is required: the desire to know this Self by turning the eyes inwards. All these beautiful things that we see in nature are very good, but that is not the way to see God. We must learn how to turn the eyes inwards. The eagerness of the eyes to see outwards should be restricted. When you walk in a busy street, it is difficult to hear the man speak with whom you are walking, because of the noise of the passing carriages. He cannot hear you because there is so much noise. The mind is going outwards, and you cannot hear the man who is next to you. In the same way; this world around us is making such a noise that it draws the mind outwards. How can we see the Self? This going outwards must be stopped. That is what is meant by turning the eyes inwards, and then alone the glory of the Lord within will be seen.

What is this Self? We have seen that it is even beyond the intellect. We learn from the same Upanishad that this Self is eternal and omnipresent, that you and I and all of us are omnipresent beings, and that the Self is changeless. Now this omnipresent Being can be only one. There cannot be two beings who are equally omnipresent — how could that be?

There cannot be two beings who are infinite, and the result is, there is really only one Self, and you, I, and the whole universe are but one, appearing as many. 'As the one fire entering into the world manifests itself in various ways, even so that one Self, the Self of all, manifests Itself in every form.' But the question is: If this Self is perfect and pure and the One Being of the universe, what becomes of It when It goes into the impure body, the wicked body, the good body, and so on? How can It remain perfect? 'The one sun is the cause of vision in every eye, yet it is not touched by the defects in the eyes of any.' If a man has jaundice he sees everything as yellow; the cause of his vision is the sun, but his seeing everything as yellow does not touch the sun. Even so this One Being, though the Self of every one, is not touched by the purities or impurities outside. 'In this world where everything is evanescent, he who knows Him who never changes in this world of insentiency, he who knows the one sentient Being in this world of many, he who knows this One and sees Him in his own soul, unto him belongs eternal bliss, to none else, to none else. There the sun shines not, nor the stars, nor the lightning flashes, what to speak of fire? He shining, everything shines; through His light everything becomes effulgent. When all the desires that trouble the heart cease, then the mortal becomes immortal, and here one attains Brahman. When all the crookedness of the heart disappears, when all its knots are cut asunder, then alone the mortal becomes immortal. This is the way. May this study bless us; may it become food to us; may it give us strength;

may it become energy in us; may we not hate each other; peace unto all!'

This is the line of thought that you will find in the Vedanta philosophy. We see first that here is a thought entirely different from what you see anywhere else in the world. In the oldest parts of the Vedas the search was the same as in other books, the search was outside. In some of the old, old books, the question was raised, 'What was in the beginning? When there was neither aught nor naught, when darkness was covering darkness, who created all this?' So the search began, and they began to talk about the angels, the Devas, and all sorts of things, and later on we find that they gave it up as hopeless. In their day the search was outside and they could find nothing; but in later days, as we read in the Vedas, they had to look inside for the Self-existent One. This is the one fundamental idea in the Vedas, that our search in the stars, the nebulae, the Milky Way, in the whole of this external universe leads to nothing, never solves the problem of life and death. The wonderful machanism inside had to be analysed, and it revealed to them the secret of the universe; no star or sun could do it. Man had to be anatomised; not the body, but the soul of man. In that soul they found the answer. What was the answer they found? That behind the body, behind even the mind, there is the Self-existent One. He dies not, nor is He born. The Self-existent One is omnipresent, because He has no form. That which has no form or shape, that which is not limited by space or time, cannot live in a certain place. How can it? It is everywhere, omnipresent, equally present through all of us.

What is the soul of man? There was one party who held that there is a being, God, and an infinite number of souls besides, who are eternally separate from God in essence and form and everything. This is dualism. This is the old, old crude idea. The answer given by another party was that the soul was a part of the infinite Divine Existence. Just as this body is a little world by itself, and behind it is the mind or thought, and behind that is the individual soul, similarly the whole world is a body, and behind that is the universal mind, and behind that is the universal Soul. Just as this body is a portion of the universal body, so this mind is a portion of the universal mind, and the soul of man a portion of the universal Soul. This is what is called the Vishishtadvaita, qualified monism. Now, we know that the universal Soul is infinite. How can infinity have parts? How can it be broken up, divided? It may be very poetic to say that I am a spark of the Infinite, but it is absurd to the thinking mind. What is meant by dividing Infinity? Is it something material that you can part or separate it into pieces? Infinity can never be divided. If that were possible, it would be no more Infinite. What is the conclusion then? The answer is, that Soul which is the universal is you; you are not a part but the whole of It. You are the whole of God. Then what are all these varieties? We find so many millions of individual souls. What are they? If the sun reflects upon millions of globules of water, in each globule is the form, the perfect image of the sun; but they are only images, and the real sun is only one. So this apparent soul that is in

every one of us is only the image of God, nothing
beyond that. The real Being, who is behind, is that one
God. We are all one there. As Self, there is only one in
the universe. It is in me and you, and is only one; and
that one Self has been reflected in all these various
bodies as various different selves. But we do not know
this; we think we are separate from each other and
separate from Him. And so long as we think this, misery
will be in the world. This is hallucination. Then the
other great source of misery is fear. Why does one man
injure another? Because he fears he will not have
enough enjoyment. One man fears that, perhaps, he will
not have enough money, and that fear causes him to
injure others and rob them. How can there be fear if
there is only one existence? If a thunderbolt falls on my
head, it was I who was the thunderbolt, because I am
the only existence. If a plague comes, it is I; if a tiger
comes, it is I. If death comes, it is I. I am both death and
life. We see that with the idea that there are two in the
universe, fear comes. We have always heard it preached,
'Love one another.' What for? That doctrine was
preached, but the explanation is here. Why should I love
every one? Because they and I are one. Why should I
love my brother? Because he and I are one. There is this
oneness, this solidarity of the whole universe. From the
lowest worm that crawls under our feet to the highest
beings that ever lived — *all* have various bodies, but are
the one Soul. Through all mouths, you eat; through all
hands, you work; through all eyes, you see. You enjoy
health in millions of bodies, you are suffering from
disease in millions of bodies. When this comes, and

we realise it, see it, feel it, then will misery cease, and fear with it. How can I die? There is nothing beyond me. Fear ceases, and then alone come perfect happiness and perfect love. That universal sympathy, universal love, universal bliss, that never changes, raises man above everything. It has no reactions, and no misery can touch it; but this little eating and drinking of the world always brings a reaction. The whole cause of it is this dualism, the idea that I am separate from the universe, separate from God. But as soon as we have realised that 'I am He, I am the Self of the universe, I am eternally blessed, eternally free' — then will come real love, fear will vanish, and all misery cease.

THE POWERS OF THE MIND

(RAJA-YOGA)

(Delivered at Los Angeles, California, Jan.8, 1900)

All over the world there has been the belief in the supernatural throughout the ages. All of us have heard of extraordinary happenings, and many of us have had some personal experience of them. I would rather introduce the subject by telling you certain facts which have come within my own experience. I once heard of a man who, if any one went to him with questions in his mind, would answer them immediately; and I was also informed that he foretold events. I was curious and went to see him with a few friends. Each one of us had something in our minds to ask and to avoid mistakes each of us wrote down our questions and put them in our pockets. As soon as the man saw one of us, he repeated our questions and gave the answers to them. Then he wrote something on paper, which he folded up, asked me to sign on the back, and said, 'Don't look at it; put it in your pocket and keep it there till I ask for it again.' And so on to each one of us. He next told us about some events that would happen to us in the future. Then he said, 'Now, think of a word or a sentence, from any language you like.' I thought of a long sentence from Sanskrit, a language of which he was entirely ignorant. 'Now, take out the paper from your pocket,' he said. The Sanskrit sentence was written there! He had written it an hour before with the remark, 'In confirmation of what I have written, this man will think of this sentence.' It was correct. Another of us who had been given a similar paper, which he had signed and placed in his pocket, was also asked to think of a sentence. He thought of a sentence in Arabic, which it was still less possible for the man to know; it was some passage from the Koran. And my friend found this written down on the paper. Another of us was a physician. He thought of a sentence from a German medical book. It was written on his paper. Several days later I went to this man again, thinking possibly I had been deluded somehow before. I took other friends, and on this occasion also he came out wonderfully triumphant.

Another time I was in the city of Hyderabad in India, and I was told of a Brahmin there who could produce numbers of things from where nobody knew. This man was in business there; he was a respectable gentleman. And I asked him to show me his tricks. It so happened that this man had a fever, and in India there is a general belief that if a holy man puts his hand on a sick man he would be well. This Brahmin came to me and said, 'Sir, put your hand on my head, so that my fever may be cured.' I said, 'Very good, but you show me your tricks.' He promised. I put my hand on his head as desired, and later he came to fulfil his promise. He had only a strip of cloth about his loins, we took off everything else from him. I had a blanket which I gave him to wrap round himself, because it was cold, and made him sit in a corner. Twenty-five pairs of eyes were looking at him. And he said, 'Now, look, write down anything you want.' We all wrote down names of fruits that never grew in that country, bunches of grapes, oranges, and so on. And we gave him those bits of paper. And there came from under his blanket, bushels of grapes, oranges, and so forth, so much that if all that fruit was weighed, it would have been twice as heavy as the man. He asked us to eat the fruit. Some of us objected, thinking it was hypnotism; but the man began eating himself — so we all ate. It was all right.

He ended by producing a mass of roses. Each flower was perfect, with dew-drops on the petals, not one crushed, not one injured. And masses of them! When I asked the man for an explanation, he said, 'It is all sleight of hand.'

Whatever it was, it seemed to be impossible that it could be sleight of hand merely. From where could he have got such large quantities of things?

Well, I saw many things like that. Going about India, you find hundreds of similar things in different places. These are in every country. Even in this country you will find some such wonderful things. Of course there is a greater deal of fraud, no doubt; but then, whenever you see fraud, you have also to say that fraud is an imitation. There must be some truth somewhere, that is being imitated; you cannot imitate nothing. Imitation must be of something substantially true.

In very remote times in India, thousands of years ago, these facts used to happen even more than they do today. It seems to me that when a country becomes very thickly populated, psychical power deteriorates. In a vast country thinly inhabited, there will, perhaps, be more of psychical power there. These facts, the Hindus, being analytically minded, took up and investigated. And they came to certain remarkable conclusions; that is, they made a science of it. They found out that all these, though extraordinary, are also natural; there is nothing supernatural. They are under laws just the same as any other physical phenomenon. It is not a freak of nature that a man is born with such powers. They can be systematically studied, practised, and acquired. This science they call the science of Raja Yoga. There are thousands of people who cultivate the study of this science, and for the whole nation it has become a part of daily worship.

The conclusion they have reached is that all these extraordinary powers are in the mind of man. This mind is a part of the universal mind. Each mind is connected with every other mind. And each mind, wherever it is located, is in actual communication with the whole world.

Have you ever noticed the phenomenon that is called thought-transference? A man here is thinking something, and that thought is manifested in somebody else, in some other place. With preparation—not by chance—a man wants to send a thought to another mind at a distance and this other mind knows that a thought is coming, and he receives it exactly as it is sent out. Distance makes no difference. The thought goes and reaches the other man, and he understands it. If your mind were an isolated something there, and my mind were an isolated something here, and there were no connection between the two, how would it be possible for my thought to reach you? In the ordinary cases, it is not my thought that is reaching you direct; but my thought has got to be dissolved into ethereal vibrations and those ethereal vibrations go into your brain, and they have to be resolved again into your own thoughts. Here is a dissolution of thought, and there is a resolution of thought. It is a roundabout process. But in telepathy there is no such thing, it is direct.

This shows that there is a continuity of mind, as the Yogis call it. The mind is universal. Your mind, my mind, all these little minds, are fragments of that universal mind, little waves in the ocean; and on account of this continuity, we can convey our thoughts directly to one another.

You see what is happening all around us. The world is one of influence. Part of our energy is used up in the preservation of our own bodies. Beyond that, every particle of our energy is day and night being used in influencing others. Our bodies, our virtues, our intellect, and our spirituality, all these are continuously influencing others; and so, conversely, we are being influenced by them. This is going on all around us. Now, to take a concrete example: A man comes — you know he is very learned, his language is beautiful, and he speaks to you by the hour; but he does not make any impression. Another man comes, and he speaks, few words, not well arranged, ungrammatical perhaps; all the same, he makes an immense impression. Many of you have seen that. So it is evident that words alone cannot always produce an impression. Words, even thoughts contribute only one-third of the influence in making an impression, the man two-thirds. What you call the personal magnetism of the man — that is what goes out and impresses you.

In our families there are the heads; some of them are successful, others are not. Why? We complain of others in our failures. The moment I am unsuccessful, I say, so and so is the cause of the failure. In failures one does not like to confess one's own faults and weakness. Each person tries to hold himself faultless and lay the blame upon somebody or something else, or even on bad luck. When heads of families fail, they should ask themselves, why it is that some persons manage a family so well and others do not. Then you will find that the difference is owing to the man — his presence, his personality.

Coming to great leaders of mankind, we always find that it was the personality of the man that counted. Now, take all the great authors of the past, the great thinkers. Really speaking, how many thoughts have they thought? Take all the writings that have been left to us by the past leaders of mankind; take each one of their books, and appraise them. The real thoughts, new and genuine, that have been thought in this world up to this time, amount to only a handful. Read in their books the thoughts they have left to us. The authors do not appear to be giants to us, and yet we know that they were great giants in their days. What made them so? Not simply the thoughts they thought, neither the books they wrote, nor the speeches they made, it was something else that is now gone, that is their personality. As I have already remarked, the personality of the man is two-thirds, and his intellect, his words, are but one-third. It is the real man, the personality of the man, that runs through us. Our actions are but effects. Actions must come when the man is there; the effect is bound to follow the cause.

The ideal of all education, all training, should be this man-making. But, instead of that, we are always trying to polish up the outside. What use in polishing up the outside when there is no inside? The end and aim of all training is to make the man grow. The man who influences, who throws his magic, as it were, upon his fellow-beings, is a dynamo of power, and when that man is ready, he can do anything and everything he likes; that personality put upon anything will make it work.

Now, we see that though this is a fact, no physical laws that we know of will explain this. How can we explain it by chemical and physical knowledge? How much of oxygen, hydrogen, carbon—how many molecules in different positions, and how many cells, etc., etc., can explain this mysterious personality? And we still see, it is a fact, and not only that, it is the real man; and it is that man that lives and moves and works; it is that man that influences, moves his fellow-beings and passes out, and his intellect and books and works are but traces left behind. Think of this. Compare the great teachers of religion with the great philosophers. The philosophers scarcely influenced anybody's inner man, and yet they wrote most marvellous books. The religious teachers, on the other hand, moved countries in their lifetime. The difference was made by personality. In the philosopher it is a faint personality that influences; in the great Prophets it is tremendous. In the former we touch the intellect, in the latter we touch life. In the one case, it is simply a chemical process putting certain chemical ingredients together which may gradually combine and under proper circumstances bring out a flash of light or may fail. In the other, it is like a torch that goes round quickly, lighting others.

The science of Yoga claims that it has discovered the laws which develop this personality, and by proper attention to those laws and methods, each one can grow and strengthen his personality. This is one of the great practical things and this is the secret of all education. This has a universal application. In the life of the householder, in the life of the poor, the rich, the man of business, the spiritual man, in everyone's life it is a great thing, the strengthening of this personality. There are laws, very fine, which are behind the physical laws, as we know. That is to say, there are no such realities as a physical world, a mental world, a spiritual world. Whatever is, is one. Let us say, it is a sort of tapering existence; the thickest part is here: it tapers and becomes finer and finer; the finest is what we call spirit; the grossest, the body. And just as it is here, in the microcosm, it is exactly the same in the macrocosm. The universe of ours is exactly like that; it is the gross external thickness, and it tapers into something finer and finer until it becomes God.

We also know that the greatest power is lodged in

the fine, not in the coarse. We see a man take up a huge weight, we see his muscles swell, and all over his body we see signs of exertion, and we think the muscles are powerful things. But it is the thin threadlike things, the nerves, which bring power to the muscles; the moment one of these threads is cut off from reaching the muscles, they are not able to work at all. These tiny nerves bring the power from something still finer, and that again in its turn brings it from something finer still — thought, and so on. So, it is the fine that is really the seat of power. Of course we can see the movements in the gross; but when fine movements take place, we cannot see them. When a gross thing moves, we catch it, and thus we naturally identify movement with things which are gross. But all the power is really in the fine. We do not see any movement in the fine, perhaps because the movement is so intense that we cannot perceive it. But if by any science, any investigation, we are helped to get hold of these finer forces which are the cause of the expression, the expression itself will be under control. There is a little bubble coming from the bottom of a lake; we do not see it coming all the time, we see it only when it bursts on the surface; so, we can perceive thoughts only after they develop a great deal, or after they become actions. We constantly complain that we have no control over our actions, over our thoughts. But how can we have it? If we can get control over the fine movements, if we can get hold of thought at the root, before it has become thought, before it has become action, then it would be possible for us to control the whole. Now, if there is a method by which we can analyse, investigate, understand, and finally grapple with those finer powers, the finer causes, then alone it is possible to have control over ourselves, and the man who has control over his own mind assuredly will have control over every other mind. That is why purity and morality have been always the object of religion; a pure, moral man has control of himself. And all minds are the same, different parts of one Mind. He who knows one lump of clay has known all the clay in the universe. He who knows and controls his own mind, knows the secret of every mind, and has power over every mind.

Now, a good deal of our physical evil we can get rid of, if we have control over the fine parts; a good many worries we can throw off, if we have control over the fine movements; a good many failures can be averted, if we have control over these fine powers. So far is utility. Yet beyond, there is something higher.

Now, I shall tell you a theory, which I will not argue now, but simply place before you the conclusion. Each man in his childhood runs through the stages through which his race has come up; only the race took thousands of years to do it, while the child takes a few years. The child is first the old savage man — and he crushes a butterfly under his feet. The child is at first like the primitive ancestors of his race. As he grows, he passes through different stages until he reaches the development of his race. Only he does it swiftly and quickly. Now, take the whole of humanity as a race or take the whole of the animal creation, man and the lower animals, as one whole. There is an end towards which the whole is moving. Let us call it perfection. Some men and women are born who anticipate the whole progress of mankind. Instead of waiting and being reborn over and over again for ages until the whole human race has attained to that perfection, they, as it were, rush through them in a few short years of their life. And we know that we can hasten these processes, if we be true to ourselves. If a number of men, without any culture, be left to live upon an island, and are given barely enough food, clothing and shelter, they will gradually go on and on, evolving higher and higher stages of civilisation. We know also that this growth can be hastened by additional means. We help the growth of trees, do we not? Left to nature they would have grown, only they would have taken a longer time; we help them to grow in a shorter time than they would otherwise have taken. We are doing all the time the same thing, hastening the growth of things by artificial means. Why cannot we hasten the growth of man? We can do that as a race. Why are teachers sent to other countries? Because by these means we can hasten the growth of race. Now, can we not hasten the growth of individuals? We can. Can we put a limit to the hastening? We cannot say how much a man can grow in one life. You have no reason to say that this much a man can do and no more. Circumstances can hasten him wonderfully. Can there be any limit then, till you come to perfection? So, what comes of it? — That a perfect man, that is to say, the type that is to come of this race, perhaps millions of years hence, that man can come today. And this is what the Yogis say, that all great incarnations and prophets are such men; that they reached perfection in this one life. We have had such men at all periods of the world's history and at all times. Quite recently, there was such a man who lived the life of the whole human race and reached the end — even in this life. Even this hastening of the growth must be under laws. Suppose we can investigate these laws and understand their secrets and apply them to our own needs; it follows that we grow. We hasten our growth, we hasten our development, and we become perfect even in this life. This is the higher part of our life, and the science of the study of mind and its powers has this perfection as its real end. Helping others with money and other material things and teaching them how to go on smoothly in their daily life are mere details.

The utility of this science is to bring out the perfect man, and not let him wait and wait for ages, just a plaything in the hands of the physical world, like a log of drift-wood carried from wave to wave and tossing about in the ocean. This science wants you to be strong, to take the work in your own hand, instead of leaving it in the hands of nature, and get beyond this little life. That is the great idea.

Man is growing in knowledge, in power, in happiness. Continuously, we are growing as a race. We see that is true, perfectly true. Is it true of individuals? To a certain extent, yes. But yet, again comes the question: Where do you fix the limit? I can see only at a distance of so many feet. But I have seen a man close his eyes and see what is happening in another room. If you say you do not believe it, perhaps in three weeks that man can make you do the same. It can be taught to anybody. Some persons, in five minutes even, can be made to read what is happening in another man's mind. These facts can be demonstrated.

Now, if these things are true, where can we put a limit? If a man can read what is happening in another's mind in the corner of this room, why not in the next room? Why not anywhere? We cannot say, why not. We dare not say that it is not possible. We can only say, we do not know how it happens. Material scientists have no right to say that things like this are not possible; they can only say, 'We do not know.' Science has to collect facts, generalise upon them, deduce principles, and state the truth — that is all. But if we begin by denying the facts, how can a science be?

There is no end to the power a man can obtain. This is the peculiarity of the Indian mind, that when anything interests it, it gets absorbed in it and other things are neglected. You know how many sciences had their origin in India. Mathematics began there. You are even today counting 1, 2, 3, etc. to zero, after Sanskrit figures, and you all know that Algebra also originated in India, and that gravitation was known to the Indians thousands of years before Newton was born.

You see the peculiarity. At a certain period of Indian history, this one subject of man and his mind absorbed all their interest. And it was so enticing, because it seemed the easiest way to achieve their ends. Now, the Indian mind became so thoroughly persuaded that the mind could do anything and everything according to law, that its powers became the great object of study. Charms, magic, and other powers, and all that, were nothing extraordinary, but a regularly science, just as the physical sciences they had taught before that. Such a conviction in these things came upon the race that physical sciences nearly died out. It was the one thing that came before them. Different sects of Yogis began to make all sorts of experiments. Some made experiments with light, trying to find out how lights of different colours produced changes in the body. They wore a certain coloured cloth, lived under a certain colour, and ate certain coloured foods. All sorts of experiments were made in this way. Others made experiments in sound by stopping and unstopping their ears. And still others experimented in the sense of smell, and so on.

The whole idea was to get at the basis, to reach the fine parts of the things. And some of them really showed most marvellous powers. Many of them were trying to float in the air or pass through it. I shall tell you a story which I heard from a great scholar in the West. It was told him by a Governor of Ceylon who saw the performance. A girl was brought forward and seated cross-legged upon a stool made of sticks crossed. After she had been seated for a time, the show-man began to take out, one after another, these cross-bars; and when all were taken out, the girl was left floating in the air. The Governor thought there was some trick, so he drew his sword and violently passed it under the girl; nothing was there. Now, what was this? It was not magic or something extraordinary. That is the peculiarity. No one in India would tell you that things like this do not exist. To the Hindu it is a matter of course. You know what the Hindus would often say when they have to fight their enemies — 'Oh, one of our Yogis will come and drive the whole lot out.' It is the extreme belief of the race. What power is there in the hand or the sword? The power is all in the spirit.

If this is true, it is temptation enough for the mind to exert its highest. But as with every other science it is very difficult to make any great achievement, so also with this, nay much more. Yet most people think that these powers can be easily gained. How many are the years you take to make a fortune? Think of that! First, how many years do you take to learn electrical science or engineering? And then you have to work all the rest of your life.

Again, most of the other sciences deal with things that do not move, that are fixed. You can analyse the chair, the chair does not fly from you. But this science deals with the mind, which moves all the time; the moment you want to study it, it slips. Now the mind is in one mood, the next moment, perhaps, it is different, changing, changing all the time. In the midst of all this change it has to be studied, understood, grasped, and controlled. How much more difficult then is this science! It requires rigorous training. People ask me why I do not give them practical lessons. Why, it is no joke. I stand upon this platform talking to you, and you go home and find no benefit; nor do I. Then you say, 'It is all bosh.' It is because you wanted to make a bosh of it. I know very little of this science, but the little that I gained I worked for thirty years of my life, and for six years I have been telling people the little that I know. It took me thirty years to learn it; thirty years of hard struggle. Sometimes I worked at it twenty hours during the twenty-four; sometimes I slept only one hour in the night; sometimes I worked whole nights; sometimes I lived in places where there was hardly a sound, hardly a breath; sometimes I had to live in caves. Think of that. And yet I know little or nothing: I have barely touched the hem of the garment of this science. But I can understand that it is true and vast and wonderful.

Now, if there is anyone amongst you who really wants to study this science, he will have to start with that sort of determination, the same as, nay even more than, that which he puts into any business of life.

And what an amount of attention does business require, and what a rigorous taskmaster it is! Even if the father, the mother, the wife, or the child dies, the business cannot stop! Even if the heart is breaking, we still have to go to our place of business, when every hour of work is a pang. That is business, and we think that it is just, that it is right.

This science calls for more application than any business can ever require. Many men can succeed in business; very few in this. Because so much depends upon the particular constitution of the person studying it. As in business all may not make a fortune, but everyone can make something, so in the study of this science each one can get a glimpse which will convince him of its truth and of the fact that there have been men who realised it fully.

This is the outline of this science. It stands upon its own feet and in its own light, and challenges comparison with any other science. There have been charlatans, there have been magicians, there have been cheats, and more here than in any other field. Why? For the same reason, that the more profitable the business, the greater the number of charlatans and cheats. But that is no reason why the business should not be good. And one thing more; it may be a good intellectual gymnastics to listen to all the arguments and an intellectual satisfaction to hear of wonderful things. But, if anyone of you really wants to learn something beyond that, merely attending lectures will not do. That cannot be taught in lectures, for it is life; and life can only convey life. If there are any amongst you who are really determined to learn it, I shall be very glad to help them.

THE OPEN SECRET

(JNANA-YOGA)

(Delivered at Los Angeles, Calif., Jan. 5, 1900)

Whichever way we turn in trying to understand things in their reality, if we analyse far enough, we find that at last we come to a peculiar state of things, seemingly a contradiction: something which our reason cannot grasp and yet is a fact. We take up something — we know it is finite; but as soon as we begin to analyse it, it leads us beyond our reason, and we never find an end to all its qualities, its possibilities, its powers, its relations. It has become infinite. Take even a common flower, that is finite enough; but who is there that can say he knows all about the flower? There is no possibility of anyone's getting to the end of the knowledge about that one flower. The flower has become infinite — the flower which was finite to begin with. Take a grain of sand. Analyse it. We start with the assumption that it is finite, and at last we find that it is not, it is infinite; all the same, we have looked upon it as finite. The flower is similarly treated as finite something.

So with all our thoughts and experiences, physical and mental. We begin, we may think, on a small scale, and grasp them as little things; but very soon they elude our knowledge and plunge into the abyss of the infinite. And the greatest and the first thing perceived is ourselves. We are also in the same dilemma about existence. We exist. We see we are finite beings. We live and die. Our horizon is narrow. We are here, limited, confronted by the universe all around. Nature can crush us out of existence in a moment. Our little bodies are just held together, ready to go to pieces at a moment's notice. We know that. In the region of action how powerless we are! Our will is being thwarted at every turn. So many things we want to do, and how few we can do! There is no limit to our willing. We can will everything, want everything, we can desire to go to the Dog Star. But how few of our desires can be accomplished! The body will not allow it. Well, nature is against the accomplishment of our will. We are weak. What is true of the flower, of the grain of sand, of the physical world, and of every thought, is a hundredfold more true of ourselves. We are also in the same dilemma of existence, being finite and infinite at the same time. We are like waves in the ocean; the wave is the ocean and yet not the ocean. There is not any part of the wave of which you cannot say, 'It is the ocean.' The name 'ocean' applies to the wave and equally to every other part of the ocean, and yet it is separate from the ocean. So in this infinite ocean of existence, we are like wavelets. At the same time, when we want really to grasp ourselves, we cannot—we have become the infinite.

We seem to be walking in dreams. Dreams are all right in a dream-mind; but as soon as you want to grasp one of them, it is gone. Why? Not that it was false, but because it is beyond the power of reason, the power of the intellect, to comprehend it. Everything in this life is so vast that the intellect is nothing in comparison with it. It refuses to be bound by the laws of the intellect! It laughs at the bondage the intellect wants to spread around it. And a thousandfold more so is this the case with the human soul. 'We ourselves' — this is the greatest mystery of the universe.

How wonderful it all is! Look at the human eye. How easily it can be destroyed, and yet the biggest suns exist only because your eyes see them. The world exists because your eyes certify that it exists. Think of the mystery! These poor little eyes! A strong light, or a pin, can destroy them. Yet the most powerful engines of destruction, the most powerful cataclysms, the most wonderful of existences, millions of suns and stars and moons and earth — all depend for their existence upon, and have to be certified by, these two little things! They say, 'Nature, you exist,' and we believe nature exists. So with all our senses.

What is this? Where is weakness? Who is strong? What is great and what is small? What is high and what is low in this marvellous interdependence of existence, where the smallest atom is necessary for the existence of the whole? Who is great and who is small? It is past finding out! And why? Because none is great and none is small. All things are interpenetrated by that infinite ocean; their reality is that infinite; and whatever there is on the surface is but that infinite. The tree is infinite; so is everything that you see or feel — every grain of sand, every thought, every soul, everything that exists, is infinite. Infinite is finite and finite infinite. This is our existence.

Now, that may be all true, but all this feeling after the Infinite is at present mostly unconscious. It is not that we have forgotten that infinite nature of ours; none can ever do that. Who can ever think that he can be annihilated? Who can think that he will die? None can. All our relation to the Infinite works in us unconsciously. In a manner, therefore, we forget our real being, and hence all this misery comes.

In practical daily life we are hurt by small things; we are enslaved by little beings. Misery comes because we think we are finite — we are little beings. And yet, how difficult it is to believe that we are infinite beings! In the midst of all this misery and trouble, when a little thing may throw me off my balance, it must be my care to believe that I am infinite. And the fact is that we are, and that consciously or unconsciously we are all searching after that something which is infinite; we are always seeking for something that is free.

There was never a human race which did not have a religion and worship some sort of God or gods. Whether the God or gods existed or not is no question; but what is the analysis of this psychological phenomenon? Why is all the world trying to find, or seeking for, a God? Why? Because in spite of all this bondage, in spite of nature and this tremendous energy of law grinding us down, never allowing us to turn to any side — wherever we go, whatever we want to do, we are thwarted by this law, which is everywhere — in spite of all this, the human soul never forgets its freedom and is ever seeking it. The search for freedom is the search of all religions; whether they know it or not, whether they can formulate it well or ill, the idea is there. Even the lowest man, the most ignorant, seeks for something which has power over nature's laws. He wants to see a demon, a ghost, a god — somebody who can subdue nature, for whom nature is not almighty, for whom there is no law. 'Oh, for somebody who can break the law!' That is the cry coming from the human heart. We are always seeking for someone who breaks the law. The rushing engine speeds along the railway track, the little worm crawls out of its way. We at once say, 'The engine is dead matter, a machine; and the worm is alive,' because the worm attempted to break the law. The engine, with all its power and might, can never break the law. It is made to go in any direction man wants, and it cannot do otherwise; but the worm, small and little though it was, attempted to break the law and avoid the danger. It tried to assert itself against law, assert its freedom; and there was the sign of the future God in it.

Everywhere we see this assertion of freedom, this freedom of the soul. It is reflected in every religion in the shape of God or gods; but it is all external yet — for those who only see the gods outside. Man decided that he was nothing. He was afraid that he could never be free; so he went to seek for someone outside of nature who was free. Then he thought that there were many and many such free beings, and gradually he merged them all into one God of gods and Lord of lords. Even that did not satisfy him. He came a little closer to truth, a little nearer; and then gradually found that whatever he was he was in some way connected with the God of gods and Lord of lords; that he, though he thought himself bound and low and weak, was somehow connected with that God of gods. Then vision came to him; thought arose and knowledge advanced. And he began to come nearer and nearer to that God, and at last found out that God and all the gods, this whole psychological phenomenon connected with the search for an all-powerful free soul, was but a reflection of his own idea of himself. And then at last he discovered that it was not only true that 'God made man after His own image,' but that it was also true that man made God after his own image. That brought out the idea of divine freedom. The Divine Being was always within, the nearest of the near. Him we had ever been seeking outside, and at last found that He is the heart of our hearts. You may know the story of the man who mistook his own heart-beat for somebody knocking at the door, and went to the door and opened it, but found nobody there, so he went back. Again he seemed to hear a knocking at the door, but nobody was there. Then he understood that it was his own heartbeat, and he had misinterpreted it as a knocking at the door. Similarly, man after his search finds out that this infinite freedom that he was placing in imagination all the time in the nature outside, is the internal subject, the eternal Soul of souls — this Reality, he himself.

Thus at last he comes to recognise this marvellous duality of existence: the subject, infinite and finite in one — the Infinite Being is also the same finite soul. The

Infinite is caught, as it were, in the meshes of the intellect and apparently manifests as finite beings, but the reality remains unchanged.

This is, therefore, true knowledge: that the Soul of our souls, the Reality that is within us, is That, which is unchangeable, eternal, ever blessed, ever free. This is the only solid ground for us to stand upon.

This, then, is the end of all death, the advent of all immortality, the end of all misery. And he who sees that One among the many, that One unchangeable in the universe of change, he who sees Him as the Soul of his soul, unto him belongs eternal peace — unto none else.

And in the midst of the depths of misery and degradation, the Soul sends a ray of light, and man wakes up and finds that what is really his, he can never lose. No, we can never lose what is really ours. Who can lose his being? Who can lose his very existence? If I am good, it is the existence first, and then that becomes coloured with the quality of goodness. If I am evil, it is the existence first, and that becomes coloured with the quality of badness. That existence is first, last, and always; it is never lost, but ever present.

Therefore, there is hope for all. None can die; none can be degraded for ever. Life is but a playground, however gross the play may be. However we may receive blows, and however knocked about we may be, the Soul is there and is never injured. We are that Infinite.

Thus sang a Vedantin, 'I never had fear nor doubt. Death never came to me. I never had father or mother: for I was never born. Where are my foes? — for I am All.

I am the Existence and Knowledge and Bliss Absolute. I am It. I am It. Anger and lust and jealousy, evil thoughts and all these things, never came to me; for I am the Existence, the Knowledge, the Bliss Absolute. I am It. I am It.'

That is the remedy for all diseases, the nectar that cures death. Here we are in this world, and our nature rebels against it. But let us repeat, 'I am It; I am It. I have no fear, nor doubt, nor death. I have no sex, nor creed, nor colour. What creed can I have? What sect is there to which I should belong? What sect can hold me? I am in every sect.'

However much the body rebels, however much the mind rebels, in the midst of the uttermost darkness, in the midst of agonising tortures, in the uttermost despair, repeat this, once, twice, thrice, ever more. Light comes gently, slowly, but surely it comes.

Many times I have been in the jaws of death, starving, footsore, and weary; for days and days I had had no food, and often could walk no farther; I would sink down under a tree, and life would seem ebbing away. I could not speak, I could scarcely think, but at last the mind reverted to the idea: 'I have no fear nor death; I never hunger nor thirst. I am It! I am It! The whole of nature cannot crush me; it is my servant. Assert thy strength, thou Lord of lords and God of gods! Regain thy lost empire! Arise and walk and stop not!' And I would rise up, reinvigorated, and here am I, living, today. Thus, whenever darkness comes, assert the reality and everything adverse must vanish. For, after all, it is but a dream. Mountain-high though the difficulties appear, terrible and gloomy though all things seem, they are but Maya. Fear not—it is banished. Crush it and it vanishes. Stamp upon it, and it dies. Be not afraid. Think not how many times you fail. Never mind. Time is infinite. Go forward: assert yourself again and again, and light must come. You may pray to everyone that was ever born, but who will come to help you? And what of the way of death from which none knows escape? Help thyself out by thyself. None else can help thee, friend. For thou alone art thy greatest enemy, thou alone art thy greatest friend. Get hold of the Self, then. Stand up. Don't be afraid. In the midst of all miseries and all weakness, let the Self come out, faint and imperceptible though it be at first. You will gain courage, and at last like a lion you will roar out, 'I am It! I am It!'

'I am neither a man, nor a woman, nor a god, nor a demon; no, nor any of the animals, plants or trees. I am neither poor nor rich, neither learned nor ignorant. All these things are very little compared with what I am: for I am It! I am It! Behold the sun and the moon and the stars: I am the light that is shining in them! I am the beauty of the fire! I am the power in the universe! For, I am It! I am It!

'Whoever thinks that I am little, makes a mistake, for the Self is all that exists. The sun exists because I declare it does, the world exists because I declare it does. Without me they cannot remain, for I am Existence, Knowledge and Bliss Absolute — ever happy, ever pure, ever beautiful. Behold, the sun is the cause of our vision, but is not itself ever affected by any defect in the eyes of anyone; even so I am. I am working through all organs, working through everything, but never does the good and evil of work attach to me. For me there is no Law, no Karma. I own the Laws of Karma. I ever was and ever am.

'My real pleasure was never in earthly things — in husband, wife, children, and other things. For I am like the infinite blue sky: clouds of many colours pass over it and play for a second; they move off, and there is the same unchangeable blue. Happiness and misery, good and evil, may envelop me for a moment, veiling the Self; but I am still there. They pass away because they are changeable. I shine, because I am unchangeable. If misery comes, I know it is finite, it must go. I alone am infinite and untouched by anything. For I am Infinite, that Eternal, Changeless Self.' — So sings one of our poets.

Let us drink of this cup, this cup that leads to everything that is immortal, everything that is unchangeable. Fear not. Believe not that we are evil, that we are finite, that we can ever die. It is not true.

'This is to be heard of, then to be thought upon, and then to be meditated upon.' When the hands work, the mind should repeat — 'I am It, I am It.' Think of It, dream of It, until It becomes bone of your bones and flesh of your flesh, until all the hideous dreams of littleness, of weakness, of misery, and of evil, have entirely vanished, and no more then can the Truth be hidden from you even for a moment.

BHAKTI OR DEVOTION

(BHAKTI-YOGA)

(Delivered in New York, February 1896)

The idea of a Personal God has obtained in almost every religion, except a very few. With the exception of the Buddhist and the Jain, perhaps all the religions of the world have the idea of a Personal God, and with it comes the idea of devotion and worship. The Buddhists and the Jains, although they have no Personal God, worship the founders of their religions in precisely the same way as others worship a Personal God. This idea of devotion and worship to some higher being who can reflect back the love to man is universal. In various religions . this love and devotion is manifested in various degrees, at different stages. The lowest stage is that of ritualism, when abstract ideas are almost impossible, and are dragged down to the lowest plane, and made concrete. Forms come into play, and along with them, various symbols. Throughout the history of the world, we find that man is trying to grasp the abstract through thought-forms, or symbols. All the external manifestations of religion — bells, music, rituals, books, and images, — come under that head. Anything that appeals to the senses, anything that helps man to form a concrete image of the abstract, is taken hold of, and worshipped.

From time to time, there have been reformers in every religion who have stood against all symbols and rituals. But vain has been their opposition, for so long as man will remain as he is, the vast majority will always want something concrete to hold on to, something around which, as it were, to place their ideas, something which will be the centre of all the thought-forms in their minds. The great attempts of the Mohammedans and of the Protestants have been directed to this one end, of doing away with all rituals, and yet we find that even with them, rituals have crept in. They cannot be kept out; after long struggle, the masses simply change one symbol for another. The Mohammedan, who thinks that every ritual, every form, image, or ceremony, used by a non-Mohammedan, is sinful, does not think so when he comes to his own temple at Caaba. Every religious Mohammedan, wherever he prays, must imagine that he is standing in the temple of Caaba. When he makes a pilgrimage there, he must kiss the black stone in the wall of the temple. All the kisses that have been imprinted on that stone, by millions and millions of pilgrims, will stand up as witnesses for the benefit of the faithful on the last day of judgement. Then, there is the well of Zimzim. Mohammedans believe that whoever draws a little water out of that well, will have his sins pardoned, and he will, after the day of resurrection, have a fresh body, and live for ever.

In others, we find that the symbology comes in the form of buildings. Protestants hold that churches are more sacred than other places. The church, as it is, stands for a symbol. Or there is the Book. The idea of the Book, to them, is much holier than any other symbol. It is vain to preach against the use of symbols, and why should we preach against them? There is no reason why man should not use symbols. They have them in order to represent the ideas signified behind them. This universe is a symbol, in and through which we are trying to grasp the thing signified, which is beyond and behind. The spirit is the goal, and not matter. Forms, images, bells, candles, books, churches, temples, and all holy symbols, are very good, very helpful to the growing plant of spirituality, but thus far and no farther. In the vast majority of cases, we find that the plant does not grow. It is very good to be born in a church, but it is very bad to die in a church. It is very good to be born within the limits of certain forms that help the little plant of spirituality, but if a man dies within the bounds of these forms, it shows that he has not grown, that there has been no development of the soul

If therefore, any one says that symbols rituals, and forms are to be kept for ever, he is wrong, but if he says, that these symbols and rituals are a help to the growth of the soul, in its low and undeveloped state, he is right. But you must not mistake this development of the soul as meaning anything intellectual. A man can be of gigantic intellect, yet, spiritually, he may be a baby. You can verify it, this moment. All of you have been taught to believe in an Omnipresent God. Try to think of it. How few of you can have any idea of what omnipresence means! If you struggle hard, you will get something like the idea of the ocean, or of the sky, or of a vast stretch of green earth, or of a desert. All these are material images, and so long as you cannot conceive of the abstract as abstract, the ideal as the ideal, you will have to resort to these forms, these material images. It does not make much difference whether these images are inside or outside the mind. We are all born idolaters, and idolatry is good, because it is in the nature of man. Who can get beyond it? Only the perfect man, the God-man. The rest are all idolaters. So long as we see this universe before us, with its forms and shapes, we are all idolaters. This is a gigantic symbol we are worshipping. He who says he is the body, is a born idolater. We are spirit, spirit that has no form or shape, spirit that is infinite, and not matter. Therefore, anyone who cannot grasp the abstract, who cannot think of himself as he is, except in and through matter, as the body, is an idolater. And yet how people fight among themselves, calling one another idolaters! In other words, each says, his idol is right, and the others' are wrong.

Therefore, we should get rid of these childish notions; we should get beyond the prattle of men who think that religion is merely a mass of frothy words, that it is only a system of doctrines; to whom religion is only a little intellectual assent or dissent; to whom religion is believing in certain words which their own priests tell them; to whom religion is something which their fore-fathers believed; to whom religion is a certain form of ideas and superstitions. We should get beyond all these, and look at humanity as one vast organism,

slowly coming towards light — a wonderful plant, slowly
unfolding itself to that wonderful truth which is called
God; and the first gyrations, the first motions, towards
this are always through matter and through ritual.

In the heart of all these ritualisms, there stands one
idea prominent above all the rest — the worship of a
name. Those of you who have studied the older forms
of Christianity, those of you who have studied the other
religions of the world, perhaps have marked, that there
is this idea with them all, the worship of a name. A
name is said to be very sacred. In the Bible we read
that the holy name of God was considered sacred
beyond compare, holy beyond everything. It was the
holiest of all names, and it was thought that this very
Word was God. This is quite true. What is this universe
but name and form? Can you think without words?
Word and thought are inseparable. Try, if any one of
you can separate them. Whenever you think, you are
doing so through word forms. The one brings the other;
thought brings the word, and the word brings the
thought. Thus the whole universe is, as it were, the
external symbol of God, and behind that stands His
grand name. Each particular body is a form, and behind
that particular body is its name. As soon as you think
of our friend so-and-so, there comes the idea of his
body, and as soon as you think of your friend's body, you
get the idea of his name. This is in the constitution of
man. That is to say, psychologically, in the mind-stuff
of man, there cannot come the idea of name without the
idea of form, and there cannot come the idea of form
without the idea of name. They are inseparable; they

are the external and the internal sides of the same wave. As such, names have been exalted and worshipped all over the world — consciously or unconsciously, man found the glory of names.

Again, we find that in many different religions, holy personages have been worshipped. They worship Krishna, they worship Buddha, they worship Jesus, and so forth. Then, there is the worship of saints; hundreds of them have been worshipped all over the world, and why not? The vibration of light is everywhere. The owl sees it in the dark. That shows it is there, though man cannot see it. To man, that vibration is only visible in the lamp, in the sun, in the moon, etc. God is omnipresent; He is manifesting Himself in every being; but for men, He is only visible, recognisable, in man. When His light, His presence, His spirit, shines through the human face, then and then alone, can man understand Him. Thus, man has been worshipping God through men all the time, and must do so as long as he is a man. He may cry against it, struggle against it, but as soon as he attempts to realise God, he will find the constitutional necessity of thinking of God as a man. So we find, that in almost every religion, these are the three primary things which we have in the worship of God — forms or symbols, names, and God-men. All religions have these, but you find that they want to fight with each other. One says, 'My name is the only name; my form is the only form; and my God-men are the only God-men in the world; yours are simply myths.' In modern times, Christian clergymen have become a little kinder, and they allow that in the older religions, the different forms of worship were fore-shadowings of Christianity, which of course, they consider, is the only true form. God tested Himself in older times, tested His powers by getting these things into shape, which culminated in Christianity. This, at least, is a great advance. Fifty years ago, they would not have said even that; nothing was true except their own religion. This idea is not limited to any religion, nation, or class of persons; people are always thinking that the only right thing to be done by others is what they themselves are doing. And it is here that the study of different religions helps us. It shows us that the same thoughts that we have been calling ours, and ours alone, were present hundreds of years ago in others, and sometimes, even in a better form of expression than our own.

These are the external forms of devotion, through which man has to pass, but if he is sincere, if he really wants to reach the truth, he goes higher than these, to a plane where forms are as nothing. Temples or churches, books or forms, are simply the kindergarten of religion, to make the spiritual child strong enough to take higher steps; and these first steps are necessary if he wants religion. With the thirst, the longing for God, comes real devotion, real Bhakti. Who has the longing? That is the question. Religion is not in doctrines, in dogmas, nor in intellectual argumentation; it is being and becoming, it is realisation. We hear so many talking about God and the soul, and all the mysteries of the universe, but if you take them one by one, and ask them, 'Have you realised God? Have you seen your Soul?' – how many can say they have? And yet they are all fighting with one another! At one time, in India, representatives of different sects met together, and began to dispute. One said that the only God was Shiva; another said, the only God was Vishnu and so on; and there was no end to their discussion. A sage was passing that way, and was invited by the disputants to decide the matter. He first asked the man who was claiming Shiva as the greatest God: 'Have you seen Shiva? Are you acquainted with Him? If not, how do you know He is the greatest God?' Then turning to the worshipper of Vishnu, he asked, 'Have you seen Vishnu?' And after asking this question to all of them, he found out that no one of them knew anything of God. That was why they were disputing so much, for had they really known, they would not have argued. When a jar is being filled with water, it makes a noise, but when it is full, there is no noise. So, the very fact of these disputations and fightings among sects shows that they do not know anything about religion. Religion, to them, is a mere mass of frothy words, to be written in books. Each one, hurries to write a big book, to make it as massive as possible, stealing his materials from every book he can lay his hands upon, and never acknowledging his indebtedness. Then he launches this book upon the world adding to the disturbance that is already existing there.

The vast majority of men are atheists. I am glad that in modern times, another class of atheists has come into existence in the Western world, I mean the materialists. They are sincere atheists. They are better than the religious atheists, who are insincere, who fight and talk about religion, and yet do not want it, never try to

realise it, never try to understand it. Remember the
words of Christ — 'Ask, and it shall be given you; seek,
and ye shall find; knock, and it shall be opened unto
you.' These words are literally true, not figures, or
fiction. They were the outflow of the heart's blood of
one of the greatest sons of God, who have ever come to
this world of ours; words which came as the fruit of
realisation, from a man who had felt and realised God
himself; who had spoken with God, lived with God, a
hundred times more intensely, than you or I see this
building. Who wants God? That is the question. Do you
think that all this mass of people in the world wants
God, and cannot get Him? That cannot be. What want
is there without its object outside? Man wants to
breathe, and there is air for him to breathe. Man wants
to eat, and there is food to eat. What creates these
desires? The existence of external things. It was the light
that made the eyes; it was the sound that made the ears.
So every desire in human beings has been created by
something which already existed outside. This desire for
perfection, for reaching the goal, and getting beyond
nature, how can it be there, until something has created
it and drilled it into the soul of man, and makes it live
there? He, therefore, in whom this desire is awakened,
will reach the goal. We want everything but God. This
is no religion that you see all around you. My lady has
furniture in her parlour, from all over the world, and
now it is the fashion to have something Japanese, so
she buys a vase, and puts it in her room. Such is religion
with the vast majority; they have all sorts of things for
enjoyment, and unless they add a little flavour of

religion, life is not all right, because society would criticise them. Society expects it; so they must have some religion. This is the present state of religion in the world.

A disciple went to his master and said to him, 'Sir, I want religion.' The master looked at the young man, and did not speak, but only smiled. The young man came every day, and insisted that he wanted religion. But the old man knew better than the young man. One day, when it was very hot, he asked the young man to go to the river with him, and take a plunge. The young man plunged in, and the old man followed him, and held the young man down under the water by force. After the young man had struggled for a while, he let him go, and asked him what he wanted most while he was under the water. 'A breath of air,' the disciple answered. 'Do you want God in that way? If you do, you will get Him in a moment,' said the master. Until you have that thirst, that desire, you cannot get religion, however you may struggle with your intellect, or your books, or your forms. Until that thirst is awakened in you, you are no better than any atheist; only the atheist is sincere, and you are not.

A great sage used to say, 'Suppose there is a thief in a room, and somehow he comes to know that there is a vast mass of gold in the next room, and that there is only a thin partition between the two rooms. What would be the condition of that thief? He would be sleepless, he would not be able to eat, or do anything. His whole mind would be on getting that gold. Do you mean to say that, if all these people really believed that the Mine of

Happiness, of Blessedness, of Glory were here, they would act as they do in the world, without trying to get God?' As soon as a man begins to believe there is a God, he becomes mad with longing to get to Him. Others may go their way, but as soon as a man is sure that there is a much higher life than that which he is leading here, as soon as he feels sure that the senses are not all, that this limited, material body is as nothing compared with the immortal, eternal, undying bliss of the Self, he becomes mad until he finds out this bliss for himself. And this madness, this thirst, this mania, is what is called the 'awakening' to religion, and when that has come, a man is beginning to be religious. But it takes a long time. All these forms and ceremonies, these prayers and pilgrimages, these books, bells, candles, and priests, are the preparations; they take off the impurities from the soul; and when the soul has become pure, it naturally wants to get to the mine of all purity, God Himself. Just as a piece of iron which had been covered with the dust of centuries, might be lying near a magnet all the time, and yet not be attracted by it, but as soon as the dust is cleared away, the iron is drawn by the magnet; so, when the human soul, covered with the dust of ages, impurities, wickednesses, and sins, after many births, becomes purified enough by these forms and ceremonies, by doing good to others, loving other beings, its natural spiritual attraction comes, it wakes up, and struggles towards God.

Yet, all these forms and symbols are simply the beginning: not true love of God. Love we hear spoken of everywhere. Every one says, 'love God.' Men do not know what it is to love; if they did, they would not talk so glibly about it. Every man says he can love, and then, in no time, finds out that there is no love in his nature. Every woman says she can love, and soon finds out that she cannot. The world is full of the talk of love, but it is hard to love. Where is love? How do you know that there is love? The first test of love is, that it knows no bargaining. So long as you see a man love another only to get something from him, you know that, that is not love; it is shopkeeping. Wherever there is any question of buying and selling, it is not love. So, when a man prays to God, 'Give me this, and give me that,' it is not love. How can it be? I offer you a prayer, and you give me something in return; that is what it is, mere shopkeeping.

A certain great king went to hunt in a forest, and there he happened to meet a sage. He had a little conversation with him, and became so pleased with him that he asked him to accept a present from him. 'No,' said the sage, 'I am perfectly satisfied with my condition; these trees give me enough fruit to eat; these beautiful pure streams supply me with all the water I want; I sleep in these caves. What do I care for your presents, though you be an emperor?' The emperor said: 'Just to purify me, to gratify me, take some present and come with me into the city.' At last the sage consented to go with the emperor, and he was taken into the emperor's palace, where there were gold, jewellery, marble, and most wonderful things. Wealth and power were manifest everywhere. The emperor asked the sage to wait a minute, while he repeated his prayer, and he went into a corner and began to pray, 'Lord, give me more wealth, more children, more territory.' In the meanwhile, the sage got up, and began to walk away. The emperor saw him going and went after him. 'Stay, sir, you did not take my present, and are going away.' The sage turned to him and said: 'Beggar, I do not beg of beggars. What can you give? You have been begging yourself all the time.' That is not the language of love. What is the difference between love and shopkeeping, if you ask God to give you this, and give you that? The first test of love is that it knows no bargaining. Love is always the giver, and never the taker. Says the child of God: 'If God wants, I give Him my everything, but I do not want anything of Him. I want nothing in this universe. I love Him, because I want to love Him, and I ask no favour in return. Who cares, whether God is almighty or not? I do not want any power from Him, nor any manifestation of His power. Sufficient for me, that He is the God of love. I ask no more questions.'

The second test is, that love knows no fear. So long as man thinks of God as a Being sitting above the clouds, with rewards in one hand, and punishments in the other, there can be no love. Can you frighten one into love? Does the lamb love the lion? The mouse, the cat? The slave, the master? Slaves sometimes simulate love, but is it love? Where do you ever see love in fear? It is always a sham. With love never comes the idea of fear. Think of a young mother in the street: if a dog barks at her, she flees into the nearest house. The next day she is in the street with her child, and suppose a lion rushes upon the child: where will be her position? Just at the mouth of the lion, protecting her child. Love conquered all her fear. So also in the love of God. Who cares whether God is a rewarder or a punisher? That is not the thought of a lover. Think of a judge when he comes home, what does his wife see in him? Not a judge, or a rewarder or a punisher, but her husband, her love. What do his children see in him? There loving father; not the punisher or a rewarder. So the children of God never see in Him a punisher or a rewarder. It is only people who have never tasted of love, that fear and quake. Cast off all fear — though these horrible ideas of God as a punisher or rewarder may have their use in savage minds. Some men, even the most intellectual, are spiritual savages, and these ideas may help them. But to men who are spiritual, men who are approaching religion, in whom spiritual insight is awakened, such ideas are simply childish, simply foolish. Such men reject all ideas of fear.

The third is a still higher test. Love is always the highest ideal. When one has passed through the first two stages, when one has thrown off all shopkeeping, and cast off all fear, one then begins to realise that love was always the highest ideal. How many times in this world we see a beautiful woman loving an ugly man! How many times we see a handsome man loving an ugly woman! What is the attraction? Lookers-on only see the ugly man, or the ugly woman, but not so the lover; to the lover the beloved is the most beautiful being that ever existed. How is it? The woman who loves the ugly man takes, as it were, the ideal of beauty which is in her own mind, and projects it on this ugly man, and what she worships and loves is not the ugly man, but her own ideal. That man is, as it were, only the suggestion, and upon that suggestion she throws her own ideal, and covers it, and it becomes her object of worship. Now, this applies in every case where we love. Many of us have very ordinary looking brothers or sisters; yet the very idea of their being brothers or sisters makes them beautiful to us.

The philosophy in the background is, that each one projects one's own ideal and worships that. This external world is only the world of suggestion. All that we see, we project out of our own minds. A grain of sand gets washed into the shell of an oyster and irritates it. The irritation produces a secretion in the oyster, which covers the grain of sand and the beautiful pearl is the result. Similarly, external things furnish us with suggestions, over which we project our own ideals, and make our objects. The wicked see this world as a perfect hell, and the good as a perfect heaven. Lovers see this world as full of love, and haters as full of hatred, fighters see nothing but strife, and the peaceful nothing but peace. The perfect man sees nothing but God. So we always worship our highest ideal, and when we have reached the point, when we love the ideal as the ideal, all arguments and doubts vanish for ever. Who cares whether God can be demonstrated, or not. The ideal can never go, because it is a part of my own nature. I shall only question the ideal when I question my own existence, and as I cannot question the one, I cannot question the other. Who cares whether God can be almighty and all-merciful at the same time, or not?

Who cares whether He is the rewarder of mankind, whether He looks at us with the eyes of a tyrant or with the eyes of a beneficent monarch? The lover has passed beyond all these things, beyond rewards and punishments, beyond fears and doubts, beyond scientific, or any other demonstration. Sufficient unto him is the ideal of love, and is it not self-evident, that this universe is but a manifestation of this love? What is it that makes atoms unite with atoms, molecules with molecules, and causes planets to fly towards each other? What is it that attracts man to man, man to woman, woman to man, and animals to animals, drawing the whole universe, as it were, towards one centre? It is what is called love. Its manifestation is from the lowest atom to the highest being; omnipotent, all-pervading, is this love attraction in the sentient and the insentient, in the particular and in the universal, is the love of God. It is the one motive power that is in the universe. Under the impetus of that love, Christ gives his life for humanity, Buddha even for an animal, the mother for the child, the husband for the wife. It is under the impetus of the same love that men are ready to give up their lives for their country, and strange to say, under the impetus of the same love, the thief steals, the murderer murders. Even in these cases, the spirit is the same, but the manifestation is different. This is the one motive power in the universe. The thief has love for gold; the love is there, but it is misdirected. So, in all crimes, as well as in all virtuous actions, behind stands that eternal love. Suppose a man writes a cheque for a thousand dollars for the poor of New York, and at the

same time, in the same room, another man forges the
name of a friend. The light by which both of them write
is the same, but each one will be responsible for the use
he makes of it. It is not the light that is to be praised or
blamed. Unattached, yet shining in everything, is love,
the motive power of the universe, without which the
universe would fall to pieces in a moment, and this
love is God.

'None, O beloved, loves the husband for the
husband's sake, but for the Self that is in the husband;
none, O beloved, ever loves the wife for the wife's
sake, but for the Self that is in the wife. None ever
loves anything else, except for the Self.' Even this
selfishness which is so condemned, is but a manifestation of the same love. Stand aside from this play, do
not mix in it, but see this wonderful panorama, this
grand drama, played scene after scene and hear this
wonderful harmony; all are the manifestation of the
same love. Even in selfishness, that self will multiply,
grow and grow. That one self, the one man, will become
two selves when he gets married; several, when he
gets children; and thus he grows until he feels the whole
world as his Self, the whole universe as his Self. He
expands into one mass of universal love, infinite
love — the love that is God.

Thus we come to what is called supreme Bhakti,
supreme devotion, in which forms and symbols fall off.
One who has reached that cannot belong to any sect,
for all sects are in him. To what shall he belong? For
all churches and temples are in him. Where is the
church big enough for him? Such a man cannot bind

himself down to certain limited forms. Where is the
limit for unlimited love, with which he has become
one? In all religions which take up this ideal of love, we
find the struggle to express it. Although we understand
what this love means, and see that everything in this
world of affections and attractions is a manifestation of
that Infinite Love, the expression of which has been
attempted by sages and saints of different nations, yet
we find them using all the powers of language,
transfiguring even the most carnal expressions into the
divine.

Thus sang the royal Hebrew sage, thus sang they of
India. 'O beloved, one kiss of Thy lips! Kissed by Thee,
one's thirst for Thee increaseth for ever! All sorrows
cease, one forgets the past, present, and future, and only
thinks of Thee alone.' That is the madness of the lover,
when all desires have vanished. 'Who cares for
salvation? Who cares to be saved? Who cares to be
perfect even? Who cares for freedom?' says the lover.
'I do not want wealth, nor even health; I do not want
beauty, I do not want intellect; let me be born again and
again, amid all the evils that are in the world; I will not
complain, but let me love Thee, and that for love's sake.'
That is the madness of love which finds expression in
these songs. The highest, most expressive, strongest,
and the most attractive human love is that between man
and woman, and therefore, that language was used in
expressing the deepest devotion. The madness of this
human love was the faintest echo of the mad love of
the saints. The true lovers of God want to become
mad, inebriated with the love of God, to become 'God

intoxicated men.' They want to drink of the cup of love which has been prepared by the saints and sages of every religion, who have poured their heart's blood into it, and in which have been concentrated all the hopes of those who have loved God without seeking reward, who wanted love for itself only. The reward of love is love, and what a reward it is! It is the only thing that takes off all sorrows, the only cup, by the drinking of which this disease of the world vanishes. Man becomes divinely mad, and forgets that he is man.

Lastly, we find that all these various systems, in the end, converge to that one point, that perfect union. We always begin as dualists. God is a separate Being, and I am a separate being. Love comes between, and man begins to approach God, and God, as it were, begins to approach man. Man takes up all the various relationships of life, as father, mother, friend, or lover; and the last point is reached when he becomes one with the object of worship. 'I am you, and you are I, and worshipping you, I worship myself, and in worshipping myself, I worship you.' There we find the highest culmination of that with which man begins. At the beginning it was love for the self, but the claims of the little self made love selfish; at the end came the full blaze of light, when that self had become the Infinite. That God who at first was Being somewhere, became resolved, as it were, into Infinite Love. Man himself was also transformed. He was approaching God, he was throwing off all vain desires, of which he was full before. With desires, vanished selfishness, and, at the apex, he found that Love, Lover, and Beloved were One.

WORK AND ITS SECRET

(KARMA-YOGA)

(*Delivered at Los Angeles, Calif., Jan. 4, 1900*)

One of the greatest lessons I have learned in my life is to pay as much attention to the means of work as to its end. He was a great man from whom I learned it, and his own life was practical demonstration of this great principle. I have been always learning great lessons from that one principle, and it appears to me that all the secret of success is there: to pay as much attention to the means as to the end.

Our great defect in life is that we are so much drawn to the ideal, the goal is so much more enchanting, so much more alluring, so much bigger in our mental horizon, that we lose sight of the details altogether.

But whenever failure comes, if we analyse it critically, in ninety-nine per cent of cases we shall find that it was because we did not pay attention to the means. Proper attention to the finishing, strengthening of the means, is what we need. With the means all right, the end must come. We forget that it is the cause that produces the effect; the effect cannot come by itself; and unless the causes are exact, proper and powerful, the effect will not be produced. Once the ideal is chosen and the means determined, we may almost let go the ideal, because we are sure it will be there, when the means are perfected. When the cause is there, there is no more difficulty about the effect, the effect is bound to come. If we take care of the cause, the effect will take care of itself. The realisation of the ideal is the effect. The means are the cause: attention to the means, therefore, is the great secret of life. We also read this in the Gita and learn that we have to work, constantly work, with all our power; to put our whole mind in the work, whatever it be, that we are doing. At the same time we must not be attached. That is to say, we must not be drawn away from the work by anything else; still, we must be able to quit the work whenever we like.

If we examine our own lives, we find that the greatest cause of sorrow is this: we take up something, and put our whole energy on it — perhaps it is a failure, and yet we cannot give it up. We know that it is hurting us, that any further clinging to it is simply bringing misery on us; still, we cannot tear ourselves away from it. The bee came to sip the honey, but its feet struck to the honey-pot and it could not get away. Again and again, we are finding ourselves in that state. That is the whole secret of existence. Why are we here? We came here to sip the honey, and we find our hands and feet sticking to it. We are caught, though we came to catch. We came to enjoy; we are being enjoyed. We came to rule; we are being ruled. We came to work; we are being worked. All the time, we find that. And this comes into every detail of our life. We are being worked upon by other minds, and we are always struggling to work on other minds. We want to enjoy the pleasure of life, and they eat into our vitals. We want to get everything from nature, but we find in the long run that nature takes everything from us — depletes us, and casts us aside.

Had it not been for this, life would have been all sunshine. Never mind! With all its failures and successes, with all its joys and sorrows, it can be one succession of sunshine, if we only are not caught.

That is the one cause of misery : we are attached; we are being caught. Therefore says the Gita: Work constantly; work, but be not attached; be not caught. Reserve unto yourself the power of detaching yourself from everything, however beloved, however much the soul might yearn for it, however great the pangs of misery you feel if you were going to leave it; still, reserve the power of leaving it whenever you want. The weak have no places here, in this life or in any other life. Weakness leads to slavery. Weakness leads to all kinds of misery, physical and mental. Weakness is death. There are hundreds of thousands of microbes surrounding us, but they cannot harm us unless we become weak, until the body is ready and predisposed to receive them. There may be a million microbes of misery, floating about us. Never mind! They dare not approach us, they have no power to get a hold on us, until the mind is weakened. This is the great fact: strength is life, weakness is death. Strength is felicity, life eternal, immortal; weakness is constant strain and misery: weakness is death.

Attachment is the source of all our pleasures now. We are attached to our friends, to our relatives; we are attached to our intellectual and spiritual works; we

are attached to external objects, so that we get pleasure
from them. What, again, brings misery but this very
attachment? We have to detach ourselves to earn joy. If
only we had power to detach ourselves at will, there
would not be any misery. That man alone will be able
to get the best of nature, who, having the power of
attaching himself to a thing with all his energy, has also
the power to detach himself when he should do so. The
difficulty is that there must be as much power of
attachment as that of detachment. There are men who
are never attracted by anything. They can never love,
they are hard-hearted and apathetic; they escape most
of the miseries of life. But the wall never feels misery;
the wall never loves, is never hurt; but it is the wall,
after all. Surely it is better to be attached and caught
than to be a wall. Therefore the man who never loves,
who is hard and stony, escaping most of the miseries of
life, escapes also its joys. We do not want that. That is
weakness, that is death. That soul has not been
awakened that never feels weakness, never feels misery.
That is a callous state. We do not want that.

At the same time, we not only want this mighty power
of love, this mighty power of attachment, the power of
throwing our whole soul upon a single object, losing
ourselves and letting ourselves be annihilated, as it
were, for other souls—which is the power of the
gods—but we want to be higher even than the gods.
The perfect man can put his whole soul upon that one
point of love, yet he is unattached. How comes this?
There is another secret to learn.

The beggar is never happy. The beggar only gets a

dole with pity and scorn behind it, at least with the thought behind that the beggar is a low object. He never really enjoys what he gets.

We are all beggars. Whatever we do, we want a return. We are all traders. We are traders in life, we are traders in virtue, we are traders in religion. Alas! we are also traders in love.

If we come to trade, if it is a question of 'buy and sell,' abide by the laws of buying and selling. There is a bad time and there is a good time; there is a rise and a fall in prices: always you expect the blow to come. It is like looking at the mirror. Your face is reflected: you make a grimace—there is one in the mirror; if you laugh, the mirror laughs. This is buying and selling, giving and taking.

We get caught. How? Not by what we give, but by what we expect. We get misery in return for our love; not from the fact that we love, but from the fact that we want love in return. There is no misery where there is no want. Desire, want, is the father of all misery. Desires are bound by the laws of success and failure. Desires must bring misery.

The great secret of true success, of true happiness, then, is this: The man who asks for no return, the perfectly unselfish man, is the most successful. It seems to be a paradox. Do we not know that every man who is unselfish in life gets cheated, gets hurt? Apparently, yes. 'Christ was unselfish, and yet he was crucified.' True, but we know that His unselfishness is the reason, the cause of a great victory—the crowning of millions upon millions of lives with the blessings of true success.

Ask nothing; want nothing in return. Give what you have to give; it will come back to you — but do not think of that now. It will come back multiplied a thousandfold — but the attention must not be on that. Yet have the power to give: give and there it ends. Learn that the whole of life is giving, that nature will force you to give. So, give willingly. Sooner or later you will have to give up. You come into life to accumulate. With clenched hands, you want to take. But nature puts a hand on your throat and makes your hands open. Whether you will it or not, you have to give. The moment you say, 'I will not,' the blow comes; you are hurt. None is there but will be compelled, in the long run, to give up everything. And the more one struggles against this law, the more miserable one feels. It is because we dare not give, because we are not resigned enough to accede to this grand demand of nature, that we are miserable. The forest is gone; but we get heat in return. The sun is taking up water from the ocean, to return it in showers. You are machine for taking and giving: you take in order to give. Ask, therefore, nothing in return; but the more you give, the more will come to you. The quicker you can empty the air out of this room, the quicker it will be filled up by the external air; and if you close all the doors and every aperture, that which is within will remain, but that which is outside will never come in, and that which is within will stagnate, degenerate, and become poisoned. A river is continually emptying itself into the ocean and is continually filling up again. Bar not the exits into the ocean. The moment you do that, death seizes you.

Be, therefore, not a beggar; be unattached. This is the most terrible task of life! You do not calculate the dangers on the path. Even by intellectually recognising the difficulties, we really do not know them until we feel them. From a distance we may get a general view of a park: well, what of that? We feel and really know it when we are in it. Even if our every attempt is a failure, and we bleed and are torn asunder, yet, through all this, we have to preserve our heart — we must assert our godhead in the midst of all these difficulties. Nature wants us to react, to return blow for blow, cheating for cheating, lie for lie, to hit back with all our might. Then it requires a super-divine power not to hit back, to keep control, to be unattached.

Every day we renew our determination to be unattached. We cast our eyes back and look at the past objects of our love and attachment, and feel how every one of them made us miserable. We went down into the depths of despondency because of our 'love'! We found ourselves mere slaves in the hands of others, we were dragged down and down! And we make a fresh determination: 'Henceforth, I will be master of myself; henceforth, I will have control over myself.' But the time comes, and the same story once more! Again the soul is caught and cannot get out. The bird is in a net, struggling and fluttering. This is our life.

I know the difficulties, tremendous they are, and ninety per cent of us become discouraged and lose heart, and in our turn, often become pessimists and cease to believe in sincerity, love, and all that is grand and noble. So, we find men who in the freshness of their lives have been forgiving, kind, simple and guileless, become in old age lying masks of men. Their minds are a mass of intricacy. There may be a good deal of external policy, possibly. They are not hot-headed, they do not speak, but it would be better for them to do so; their hearts are dead and, therefore, they do not speak. They do not curse, nor become angry; but it would be better for them to be able to be angry, a thousand times better, to be able to curse. They cannot. There is death in the heart, for cold hands have seized upon it, and it can no more act, even to utter a curse, even to use a harsh word.

All this we have to avoid: therefore I say, we require superdivine power. Superhuman power is not strong enough. Superdivine strength is the only way, the one way out. By it alone we can pass through all these intricacies, through these showers of miseries, unscathed. We may be cut to pieces, torn asunder, yet our hearts must grow nobler and nobler all the time.

It is very difficult, but we can overcome the difficulty by constant practice. We must learn that nothing can happen to us, unless we make ourselves susceptible to it. I have just said, no disease can come to me until the body is ready; it does not depend alone on the germs, but upon a certain predisposition which is already in the body. We get only that for which we are fitted. Let us give up our pride and understand this, that never is misery undeserved. There never has been a blow undeserved; there never has been an evil for which I did not pave the way with my own hands. We ought to know that. Analyse yourselves and you will find that every blow you have received, came to you because you prepared yourselves for it. You did half and the external world did the other half: that is how the blow came. That will sober us down. At the same time, from this very analysis will come a note of hope, and the note of hope is: 'I have no control of the external world, but that which is in me and nearer unto me, my own world is in my control. If the two together are required to make a failure, if the two together are necessary to give me a blow, I will not contribute the one which is in my keeping and how then can the blow come? If I get real control of myself, the blow will never come.'

We are all the time, from our childhood, trying to lay the blame upon something outside ourselves. We are always standing up to set right other people, and not ourselves. If we are miserable, we say, 'Oh, the world is a devil's world.' We curse others and say, 'What infatuated fools!' But why should we be in such a world, if we really are so good? If this is a devil's world, we must be devils also; why, else, should we be here? 'Oh, the people of the world are so selfish!' True enough; but why should we be found in that company, if we be better? Just think of that.

We only get what we deserve. It is a lie when we say, the world is bad and we are good. It can never be so. It is a terrible lie we tell ourselves.

This is the first lesson to learn: be determined not to curse anything outside, not to lay the blame upon anyone outside, but be a man, stand up, lay the blame on yourself. You will find, that is always true. Get hold of yourself.

Is it not a shame that at one moment we talk so much of our manhood, of our being gods — that we know everything, we can do everything, we are blameless, spotless, the most unselfish people in the world; and at the next moment a little stone hurts us, a little anger from a little Jack wounds us — any fool in the street makes 'these gods' miserable! Should this be so if we are such gods? Is it true that the world is to blame? Could God, who is the purest and the noblest of souls, be made miserable by any of our tricks? If you are so unselfish, you are like God. What world can hurt you? You would go through the seventh hell unscathed, untouched. But the very fact that you complain and want to lay the blame upon the external world shows that you feel the external world — the very fact that you feel shows that you are not what you claim to be. You only make your offence greater by heaping misery upon misery, by imagining that the external world is hurting you, and crying out, 'Oh, this devil's world! This man hurts me; that man hurts me!' and so forth. It is adding lies to misery.

We are to take care of ourselves; that much we can do — and give up attending to others, for a time. Let us perfect the means; the end will take care of itself. For the world can be good and pure, only if our lives are good and pure. It is an effect, and we are the means. Therefore, let us purify ourselves. Let us make ourselves perfect.